Secrets of
Closing Sales

Fifth Edition

SECRETS OF CLOSING SALES

Fifth Edition

Charles B. Roth
and
Roy Alexander

Prentice-Hall, Inc.
Englewood Cliffs, N.J.

Prentice-Hall International, Inc., *London*
Prentice-Hall of Australia, Pty. Ltd., *Sydney*
Prentice-Hall Canada, Inc., *Toronto*
Prentice-Hall of India Private Ltd., *New Delhi*
Prentice-Hall of Japan, Inc., *Tokyo*
Prentice-Hall of Southeast Asia Pte. Ltd., *Singapore*
Whitehall Books, Ltd., Wellington, *New Zealand*

Library of Congress Cataloging in Publication Data

Roth, Charles B.
  Secrets of closing sales.

  Includes index.
  1. Selling.   I. Alexander, Roy
II. Title.
HF5438.25.R67   1982   658.8'5   82-12312
ISBN 0-13-797910-X

Printed in the United States of America

How This Fifth Edition
Will Aid Your Career

For nearly 40 years, Charles B. Roth's famous Master Closing Formula has helped professional salespeople *close* sales.

This book has become a classic because, without the close, *there is no sale*! Every selling professional has invested hours in prospecting, appointment-setting, and customer research only to see it all go down the drain when *the close goes awry*. Learning new and better ways to close sales is a vital and continuing need for salesfolk.

In this Fifth Edition, I've expanded—with respect and awe—Roth's tested formula. In four decades of *Secrets*, changes in products, economic conditions, industries, and social attitudes have been duly marked. Additions in this edition reflect the rise of consumerism, changed attitudes toward business, dramatic growth of service sectors of the economy.

Among other developments, today's salesperson must be prepared for larger numbers of value-aware/cost-conscious buyers—brought about by the energy shortage and rampant inflation—as well as shifting scientific and technological developments and new legal requirements. This new edition is also attuned to important social changes—particularly the women's movement. Women have rightly become a growing and valuable force in selling.

Economic conditions, new legal requirements, rapid pace of social and technological change have complicated buying decisions. They give your customer more reason for delay. They provide added reasons for a negative decision.

As a result of these changes, the Roth classic is more useful today than ever. In this book, you'll discover how to use the

Master Closing Formula to focus on the hardest part of selling—*getting the buyer to say Yes now.*

You'll master seven major closing keys and thirteen special keys—a formidable arsenal to flatten the most stubborn buyer alive.

You'll learn how prospects tell *you* when to close—and exactly how to spot *I'm-ready* signals.

In reading this book, you'll learn:

- When to let others do your closing for you
- Why storytelling signs up prospects
- How and when to sell tough in closing
- Why you should assume the no-minded buyer doesn't understand
- When to use shock treatment
- Closing when you've forgotten the sales story
- Scotching chronic-telephonitis in a buyer—and closing
- When to go back to block/tackle/run tactics

Words nail down sales—the *right* words, properly presented—and you'll take a leaf from dialogues of champion closers. You'll revel in the two most powerful words for getting A and B to come to terms—when you're in the middle.

You'll see how to improve your speech to improve your closing. You'll find out how to digest product benefits into closing power phrases. You'll learn to use words that move mountains.

You'll discover the six most powerful closing words in the American language and how to shun clichés that turn off sales. In the process, you'll see good exhibits to emulate and bad examples to avoid.

This book will also tell you how to close sales by saying "nothing" strategically, and how to use social situations to close the big ones.

Practical human-relations know-how closes sales. You'll learn to analyze four basic customer types—what to say to each, and when. To nail this ability down, you'll see how champions close with this knowledge.

You'll also learn:

- Ways to measure buyer weakness to nail down orders
- How to spot attitude shifts that lead to sign-ups
- When to turn on heat with ego-involved prospects
- How an ace salesman translates benefits into money

You'll also find out how to handle difficult buyers—opening and then closing The Clam, shutting down The Chatterbox with a buy order, bringing out dollar signs in The Money-Minded.

You'll learn how to make The Contrary sit down and sign the form, how to sell the prospect whose health will not permit him to buy, what to say when the buyer says "Absolutely not"—and means it.

You'll be amused at pusher techniques from an old carny hand. You'll learn to nail down sales so they stay closed, and the happy way of converting an awkward situation into a close.

You'll make calls with masters to share:

- One famous saleswoman's enduring secret for closing
- A famous insurance salesman's formula—and how to use it with your product
- How Swifty Lazar sells million dollar deals
- Why Columbo has more to teach you than James Bond
- How Dick Considine uses the dramatic gesture to close sales
- Why successful salespeople are part actor
- How you can profit from what poker and selling have in common
- How Bob Carl sold the world's richest man—and what you can adapt from the experience
- When to become deaf to price objections
- Getting the *mañana* buyer off the dime
- When to dominate the buyer
- Overcoming order-blank fear

You'll also learn:

- Why professional seller must match professional buyer
- Why nine out of ten salespeople insist on laying a solid foundation—then closing

- How to harness the six basic buying motivations to sign customers
- The power of listening for buying signals and then moving in for the kill
- Why Avoid Loss sells more than Get Benefit
- How to develop empathy so strong the buyer wants to buy now
- How to unearth real objections to win the order

You'll also find out the customer isn't always right—and when to tell him so to close. Action is a closer, sometimes you take it—sometimes the customer does. You'll learn *which* to do *when*. Why you should avoid eye contact while you're writing the order. Ways to use courage and audacity as allies in signing up customers. When gratitude and flattery win and when they do not.

Sometimes asking for larger order works. Sometimes you scale down. Each way closes sales—and you'll learn both.

You'll learn how to pick Mr. Right in a group and play to him—without neglecting the others. Watch a master sell two partners, playing each against the other to his advantage.

Handling competition will be easier after you watch Gayle Freeland deftly decapitate her famous competitor—as she writes the order.

As you can see, this is a treasure house of valuable, useful information. You'll find yourself referring again and again to this classic—updated and expanded—the most comprehensive treatment of closing sales ever published.

The Roth Formula can transform the novice into a full-bodied professional, make the seasoned professional's work easier and more productive, help increase income many times over for salespeople in all categories.

The Master Closing Formula will enable you to double your selling income through better handling of prospects in dozens of situations.

Put the new *Secrets of Closing Sales* to work for you. Its benefits are yours for the asking.

Roy Alexander

Acknowledgments
and
Recommended Reading

Basic acknowledgment, of course, must go to Charles B. Roth, who provided the pattern for *Secrets of Closing Sales*. Much of his basic structure and many examples remain. He was the prime mover for this book.

Other fundamental sources are recommended for further investigation and reading:

1. *Marketing Times* business update for the management professional, is published every 60 days by Sales and Marketing Executives International, 330 W. 42 Street, New York, NY 10036. Although MT covers the broad spectrum of marketing, much attention is devoted to selling as a discipline.

MT contributors that also appear in this book are Walter H. Johnson, Jr., William J. Tobin, Samuel S. Susser, Joe Gary, Robert Connolly, O.C. Halyard, Jr., Mary Kay Ash, Art Harris, Robert Carl, Dr. Paul Mok, Glenn O. Benz, David Sandler, Don Covington, Kenneth B. Haas, Peter Hockstein, Dr. Vincent S. Flowers, and Dr. Charles C. Hughes.

Another MT contributor, George Kahn (127 Echo Lake Road, Watertown, CT), publishes a series of useful monographs on selling that you may want to investigate.

2. No library on master salesmanship is complete without

- *Mehdi: Nothing Is Impossible*, the story of an immigrant who became his company's top insurance salesman. (Farnsworth Publishing Company, 78 Randall Avenue, Rockville Centre, L.I., NY.)
- *How to Master the Art of Selling* by Tom Hopkins, Champion Press, Scottsdale, AR.

3. Richard Considine, Lincoln Logs, Ltd., Gristmill Road, Chestertown, NY, believes in the selling process and is generous with his time to fellow professionals—particularly those involved with housing.

4. Al Wall, national sales manager of The MaLeck Group,

Wingate, NC, is an expert on managing manufacturers' reps and on closing sales in decorative home accessories.

5. Hubert Bermont, Bermont Books, Inc., 815 Fifteenth Street, Washington, DC 20005, publishes a series of books particularly valuable to sellers of consulting services. His books are available only by mail.

6. Dr. Paul Mok is president of Paul Mok & Associates, Dallas-based sales and sales management training firm. More details on his helpful Relationships in Selling Kit are available from him at 14455 Webb Chapel Road, Dallas, TX 75234.

The final acknowledgment must go to my colleague Connie Jason, managing editor of *Marketing Times*. Her advice and counsel in all aspects of this book have been invaluable.

R.A.

Table of Contents

IF YOU CAN'T CLOSE, YOU CAN'T SELL

1

JIM HALBERT took a clerical job in the payroll department of a large computer manufacturer. One of the first checks he processed was for $16,000.

Jim, curious, asked an older man in the department: "The man getting this check. What does he do for the company?"

"He's our top salesman," Jim was told.

"Does he get a $16,000 check every week?"

"Well, not every week. But you'd be surprised at the big ones he does get. It'd knock your eyes out."

"It already has," retorted Jim. "What are the chances of me transferring to the sales department?"

The boss of the payroll department was sympathetic though not encouraging. If Jim wanted to cut off his weekly paycheck and work on straight commission, it could probably be arranged. He promised to get Jim into the sales training program.

The first thing Jim did was to seek out the $16,000 earner and ask exactly how he did it.

"It is very easy," the successful salesman said. "All you

have to do is to circulate, see the people, tell your story, be pleasant—and always be in there trying to close the sale."

Today, Jim Halbert, still a young man, is one of the nation's most successful computer salesmen.

When Jim started selling, competitors were getting 90 percent of the business in the territory. Now Jim is getting 90 percent, competitors 10.

The leading competitor salesman, his socks knocked off, quit and went into another field. Jim literally drove his competitors out of business.

HIS SECRET: CLOSING ABILITY

You may wonder how a young upstart, selling a highly intricate and sophisticated product, with leasing contracts running around $10,000 a month and outright sales of $250,000 to $500,000, could achieve such a miracle.

To Jim Halbert, it is not a miracle. Nor is it to me. We both know what happened: Jim mastered the most important phase of salesmanship—he learned how to close.

Being successful in salesmanship is as simple as that: learn how to close and the world is yours.

Suppose a salesperson leaped over the counter of a retail store, tried on a few different jobs for size, and finally decided on a really tough field—selling encyclopedias.

Suppose in just a few years he succeeded so well he became top man in his division, then in the nation, then in the world. Suppose he could close five sales out of every six presentations. That man would have something every other salesperson needs to learn—don't you think?

There is such a salesman and his name is Robert Pachter. For years he has been either first or second in the world in his kind of selling.

Bob Pachter is one of the greatest closers of all time. Closing is his secret—what he lives for. He doesn't see any sense in making a sales call without getting the order.

So, Bob Pachter has built his entire selling approach on closing, closing, closing. The only time he fails—one time in six, remember—is when the prospect isn't a prospect in the first place.

"Give me a person who qualifies as a real prospect and I will sell him," says this ingratiating man, truthfully.

BOB BAXTER'S CLOSE

Robert E. Baxter, of Los Angeles, sells long-term industrial leases to heads of large firms. It is a tough field. But Baxter, using the most rudimentary of closing knowledge and techniques, has succeeded mightily.

Baxter's firm sent him to London to conduct negotiations for a Los Angeles skyscraper. Would American closing methods work on British real estate people? Everyone knows you can't treat the two nationalities alike. The British have more reserve, and so forth, and so forth.

But Baxter found his London clients wonderful. They responded to his American techniques. By using the simplest of selling principles, Baxter closed more sales in a year's time than he had ever closed during the preceding 25 years.

Most salespeople, however, are very poor closers. Pachter's firm has 5,000 salespeople.

"Of these, how many would you guess are in the money?" he asked me.

"Offhand, knowing the quality of the salesmen you can attract, I'd say 1,000," I replied.

"This is going to shock you," said he, "but the answer is only 200 out of 5,000. The rest I don't call salesmen at all. I call them arms and legs. They barely get by. Do you know why? They aren't closers."

Is closing sales so difficult that only 200 out of 5,000 can master it? No. To close isn't difficult. To close is the simplest, most obvious step of the sale. All it requires is first, the right attitude, and second, the right closing key. Both of these selling principles will become yours by reading this book.

Sometimes the close requires a complete summing up. H. D. Gardner, top salesman and sales counselor, was giving his presentation to Carlos Gonzalez, head of a large firm—a man who employed 100 driver-salespeople. What Gardner was selling (a sales stimulation service) would come to several thousand dollars.

Gonzalez said if Gardner could convince his two sales managers they needed the service, he would buy. Gardner went to the sales managers. They refused to buy because the boss had *secretly* told them not to buy.

What a pickle! Gardner, a courageous salesperson, went to Gonzalez, his primary prospect, and said: "Am I correct in assuming that even if your sales managers recommend my program, you won't buy it?"

On the spot, Gonzalez said: "I didn't realize how expensive it was. Our budget won't allow it."

Gardner knew he had to do something out of the ordinary. So he forgot the sale and asked Gonzalez how he had started the business (always a good idea). Gardner was looking for a peg to hang a different kind of close on.

He found it. Gonzalez, a Hispanic, had come to the United States as a young man. He had worked hard. But he never forgot his compatriots across the border. In fact, he'd given many of them jobs. Gardner picked up on this in his new close.

"That's a fascinating story, but I wonder if you haven't overlooked one thing? You've been good to Hispanics. You've hired many of them. But have you given those that work here all materials they need for success? Have you given them enough help to put them on a par with competitors? It's the one thing they lack."

Gonzalez said: "Wait a minute. I am going to buy your program."

Gardner closed on a keynote based on his customer's experience. But he had also put a foundation under his close. It was a master closing technique, but not so simple as this next one.

A San Francisco insurance sales manager, thinking to get business from the Chinese, hired a Chinese salesman. The new man broke all records.

The manager asked his new salesman the secret.

"No secret," the Oriental closer said. "I go to see China boy and ask, 'You got insurance?' If he say no, I hand him application blank and say: 'Damned fool, sign here.'"

Simplistic as this sounds, it illustrates a principle: boldness often wins.

COURAGE AND AUDACITY

What Lord Chesterfield defined as "a decent boldness" is a priceless ingredient in closing sales.

Robert Connolly tells how Arnold Gibb, a religious book sales manager, got permission to put up a book display on church property. Dr. Marble, the pastor, had remained adamant against Gibb's salesman. He wouldn't say yes.

Gibb decided to boldly force the truth.

"Dr. Marble," he said, "we find that pastors who refuse to allow a display refuse for one of two reasons. Either they hate to see money for these books leave their congregation, or they're worried about improper behavior on the part of our salespeople.

"Now you can see George Johansen, my salesrep, is a perfect gentleman. So you have no worries on that score. Further, there won't be more than a couple hundred dollars leaving your congregation. Surely this isn't enough to cause major concern."

He paused and waited for the pastor to speak. Dr. Marble blinked once and said:

"Well, I'm not worried about your man. I'm not worried about the money. You can have your display."

Dr. Marble reversed his decision rather than allow Gibb to think his motives were so negative. Courage had won the day.

Bob Pachter proved it a different way.

Pachter was trying to close a husband and wife for an expensive set of books. The prospect began writing down what Pachter was saying.

Abruptly, Pachter asked: "What are you writing?"

"The points you are making."

"Put down your pencil and paper," Pachter advised. "These things are all covered in the order blank. Why not sign it now?"

And the prospects did just that.

Courage implies the willingness to risk failure as a condition of striving for success. Theodore Roosevelt said it this way:

> Far better it is to dare mighty things, to win glorious triumphs, even though checkered by failure, than to take

rank with those poor spirits who neither enjoy much nor suffer much, because they live in the gray twilight that knows not victory nor defeat.

SELLER VS. BUYER

Closing sales requires professional application. You're dealing with sophisticates who know all the tricks and the answers. You must be a better salesperson than they are buyers.

Charles Mandel, publisher and selling force at *Science Digest,* has been an ace space salesman for 25 years. He still recalls his rocky beginning—and the lesson he learned about matching professional selling to professional buying.

"My first job was selling advertising when I was 18," Mandel relates. "One day I went back to the office and gave my sales manager a long list of excuses about why people weren't buying. The sales manager said: 'They're professional buyers. You're a professional seller. So how come they're not buying and you're not selling?'

"It's now my 25th anniversary in selling. That one remark is the basis for the most constructive attitude I could possibly have.

"Actually, sales calls to me are an upper. I enjoy them. I enjoy going out and saying, 'Hi, I don't believe you know me. My name is Charlie Mandel. Let me tell you what we're doing today.' That's fun.

"Even if I went out one day and the first six people I called on didn't buy, I would go on the seventh call exactly the same way I started the first call. I know I'd have the averages working for me. I've been doing it for so long, I know it works.

"There are people who say they wouldn't buy from me, no matter what. They think my product doesn't fit. Or they think I have bad breath. Although I miss more times than I hit, I hit many more times than most salesmen. In this business, you must be willing to miss as well as hit."

NEVER NEGLECT CLOSE

The top secret of closing more sales: be willing to *try* to close all sales. You'll keep coming back to that as you get into details on the closing keys in this book.

Into my office not long ago walked an impressive man selling a product I buy often. His firm was new to me. I listened to him courteously and attentively. I watched him carefully, as I do every salesman. This man had mastered all phases of his business. He told his story simply, convincingly, succinctly. I liked him.

But then he let me down, drastically and disappointingly. He reached the point where the close was in order. He did nothing.

To test him I asked: "Is there anything else you want to tell me about your products?"

"Why, no, I think not."

"Then it's up to me to buy or not to buy," said I.

"If you put it that way, I guess you're right."

In other words, he put his fate in my hands. I was the judge, the jury, the arbiter, the master of his fate. If I decided to buy, fine and dandy. If I didn't, what more could he do but tell his buddies that you can't trust prospects any more. They are unreliable. Selling is getting tougher every day.

Don't think for a minute this salesman is the exception. On he contrary, he is the rule. Most salespeople go about their business hoping for orders and getting some. But they never reach the full potential of what they could do.

The plain truth is that a salesperson who cannot go out and close sales, which seldom close themselves, who cannot make up customers' minds for them, who cannot overcome their procrastination, and who cannot bring in orders, isn't a salesperson at all. He or she isn't equipped to bear the name. They are business visitors or conversationalists. Who needs those?

The way a salesperson learns to become a closing specialist is by acquiring the correct habits—the practical rules that cause people to respond instantly and favorably. Perfect and practice these rules until they are a part of your everyday selling equipment. Only then do you go out as a strong closer. Only then do you make sales easily, naturally, inevitably.

The closing rules you will learn from this book are not one

person's rules. Nor do they come out of the experience of one career. They come from thousands of interviews and tests by thousands of men and women. They are a pooling of millions of hours. In this book you find them classified by situation and need, in a form you can easily acquire and use.

THE NO-WORK RATIONALE

Many salespeople won't pay the price to close all the time. More typical is George Edwards. He closed an important deal for $50,000. So he decided to celebrate. He took the day off.

"How come you're not hitting the ball, Ed?" his manager asked. "This isn't a holiday, you know."

"It is for me."

"How come?"

"I had the biggest day of my life yesterday," he explained. "Closed the Patterson Company for $50,000. I am taking a day to celebrate."

George had just talked himself out of the champion class.

You can always find a reason *not* to work. Most people are adept at it.

Wisconsin winters are not exactly Miami Beach. In a week when the temperature didn't rise much above zero, a Wisconsin salesman had a field day. He had an excuse not to work. So he goofed around the house for 13 days and didn't make a call.

"There's no use calling," he told me. "Nobody works when it's this cold."

Yet I checked retail sales and bank clearing in his city during that period. No change. Only my salesman showed a drop-off.

Like the proud mother said in watching her son's military parade in review: "Everyone's out of step except Jim!"

Another reason salespeople find for not closing more sales: they fancy themselves in a slump. The dictionary defines slump as "a mental collapse." Salespeople almost always cause it themselves. Don't lose the sale in your mind. Remember Shakespeare's advice. As Hamlet said: "There is nothing either good or bad, but thinking makes it so."

RULE OF THREE

This book follows the rule of three in teaching you to close more sales:

1. You learn the principle behind the close.
2. You dig into the practice behind the principle.
3. You get usable examples of how others have used each principle in closing sales.

As a result you'll acquire a sound, substantial knowledge of the secrets great salespeople use to close sales. Their experience will become part of your selling life. You will acquire the first essential to closing sales—confidence—in good times or bad.

Philip D. Armour, a master salesman, was also a master business-builder. He was asked: "When should you push hardest for business—when sales are easy to make and business is good, or when they are hard and business is bad?"

Said Armour: "A salesman should push hardest for sales all the time. When business is good, because it's easy to make sales. When business is bad, because then a salesman has to push hard to make any sales at all."

There's one other essential you must have, aside from knowing how to close. It is to *desire* a close—a desire so strong that everything in your life is insignificant in comparison. That desire is something you can't get from any outside source. It has to come from inside.

It's the kind of spirit that made a friend say: "There is nothing I'd rather do than sell. The prospect of closing a sale is smoke to my nostrils."

It was, too. Even after he had all the money he wanted, all the fame he could use, he was still eager to make sales. There was something about closing sales that made it the most fascinating venture in the world. His desire to sell, sell, sell was the main ingredient in his success.

BEWARE OF LOW AIM

A veteran sales manager agreed with the importance of

desire to close but added: "You haven't explained how *much* the person must want to sell. That's as important as the desire to sell in the first place.

"I want each person on my salesforce not only to want to sell, but want to sell more than any other salesperson has ever sold. I want my salespeople to get all the business in the world."

He was serious.

"The one thing I will not condone in people is low aim. By that I mean lack of ambition and the tendency to be easily satisfied. I want my people to carry the feeling that no matter how much they have sold, it isn't half enough. I want them to aim so high, to set a goal so clearly beyond themselves or anyone else, that it's the most challenging thing in their lives."

How did this sales manager get his people to accomplish that? He showed a picture of the striking statue by Phillip Sears of an Indian brave shooting arrows at the stars.

Each man or woman who comes to work for my friend gets a copy of this picture. It is a symbol of their objectives.

"I tell my people," said he, "that this statue is the very essence of success—an aspiration so high, a goal so far away, that it's like shooting an arrow at the stars. Believe me, high aim is what makes sales records."

I know it does—when you make your goals come closer by adding on large portions of know-how and selling moxie.

Walter H. Johnson, Jr., chairman of Quadrant Marketing Counselors, put this skill-acquisition process in this perspective:

> Salespersons are unique in the American business community in that they are the last great unsupervised element of the work force. The salesperson's success depends upon his or her attitude, preparation, skill and professionalism.
>
> The American standard of living and the growth and success of American business is, to a high degree, due to the unique concepts of selling—the product of our business system and our buyer's economy.
>
> One of the basic principles which runs through all of selling is the fact that all professional salesmanship is built

upon a common set of guidelines. Whether the product is highly technical, a major labor saver, or an exciting consumer product, successful sales calls follow a logical pattern of presentation and persuasion.

Contrary to a common cliché, there are no born doctors, dentists, lawyers, accountants, or salespeople. The successful salesperson has studied the craft, understands customers and their needs, and builds a presentation of product or service to meet these needs.

We live in a world of change. The customer changes daily, the product changes constantly. The salesperson must adjust psychologically and professionally to these changes.

The salesperson lives and works on the edge of change—but through all this changing world certain elements of professional principles are common and unchanged.

Most important of all: the salesperson must be familiar with the classic principles of closing sales.

In the very next chapter, you're going to start by getting the musts of closing sales.

YOUR FOUNDATION FOR
CLOSING SALES

2

JUST before the salesman went through the downstairs doors, he put his hand on my arm and said: "Let's stop here a minute. I want to prepare my thoughts."

"For success, of course!"

"No, for failure. I've been calling on this guy for 15 years and I haven't cracked him yet. He's got the Indian sign on me. Well, let's go in and get it over with."

That's the attitude of many salespeople—they prepare to fail, and fail they generally do. In every great closer, however, you can see exactly the opposite attitude: expectant success. Great closers know, just *know*, they'll sell. The first must in closing more sales is your attitude of success.

ATTITUDE CONTROLS PROGRESS

In selling, you go as far as your positive attitude will take you. You've heard about positive thinking before—and probably dismissed it as hogwash. At times, you've felt like the salesman advised to "cheer up, things could be worse." (He cheered up—and they got worse).

But to close more sales, you simply must condition your-self to believe you *will* close sales—call it positive thinking or call it confidence or call it self-esteem.

Two of the greatest closers, K.D. Kennedy and Ben Matlick, were high prophets of positive thinking. Kennedy, one of the best of his generation, said: "I enter every interview feeling no buyer was ever born who could refuse to buy from me."

Matlick, greatest closer in his field, primed his pump every morning before his first call by repeating over and over: "Today I am going to sell every prospect I see. Today I am going to close."

Imagine two salesmen. Both work hard. Both have ambi-tion. But one always expects the worst—and gets it. The other expects the best—and gets that.

The first, George Gloom, does fine till his first turndown. His courage oozes out. He becomes negative. To his credit, he keeps going in spite of it. But he is never happy or successful, and he has ulcers.

The second, Joe Joy, never gives defeat a thought. If he loses an order, he's lost an order. He will surely sell at the next call. His attitude is unfluctuating, always positive expectation. He has no ulcers.

The difference? Give it your own name. Some call it positive thinking.

CHAMPION'S CONCEPT

All great closers think and act like champions. They don't always win, but they win often enough to be champions. They're seldom discouraged and never whipped.

When J.P. Barry started selling, just out of the navy, he knew nothing about closing. He went 40 days without his first order.

At no time did he lose heart. Then things turned. He sold a $50,000 order. It put him into the running—and he hasn't stopped in 40 years. But he was a champ before he started winning. So naturally he stayed that way.

This chapter, then, is your prep school before you move on to the invaluable major and special closing keys. Here you'll learn the value of positive thinking, the importance of clear communications, and the value of "push" which an old pro picked up at a carnival. Let's start with the foundation.

BUILDING A FOUNDATION

In addition to the proper attitude, you need to put a foundation under every sale. This means making sure your customer understands precisely what you are saying. Clear understanding is the first secret of closing more sales.

A survey asked 1,000 salespeople earning $60,000 a year (and up) to explain their secrets of closing. The majority reported they closed once they were sure the prospect understood—when the foundation was in place.

Most failures to close trace back to a fuzzy or imperfect understanding.

You're talking to a prospect. You've mastered your presentation. You deliver it impressively without a hitch. *You* know all about your product or service. But does your prospect? The buyer may not possess strong intellect, may be unable to juggle new facts, especially about technical processes. Maybe you aren't getting through to the prospect at all!

He may be like my foreign-born prospect. His English was poor. I wasn't smart enough to fit my presentation to his capacities. At the end of five minutes, he said to me: "I no get. I no buy. Goodbye." I lost the sale.

FIT TO BUYER UNDERSTANDING

As long as there's the slightest misunderstanding, there's no close. No one buys an uncertainty. Make everything clear in words, pictures, diagrams, figures. Ask questions. Make every presentation primerlike.

What's the hazard of not putting a closing foundation under your sale? You lose orders and don't know why. Rarely will a customer admit to being dumb, uncomprehensive, or unable to understand. Not only will pride prevent these confessions, the buyer may not know these things in the first place.

Your job is to make sure the buyer cannot misunderstand. Remember the combat general's motto: "Whatever can be misunderstood will be misunderstood."

How do you make closing absolutely understandable?

J.E. Kennedy, a pioneer in mass selling, said every presentation should be in the language of primers used by five- and six-year-olds—everything simple, everything in one-syllable words when possible.

"Clear language is the language which carries the most conviction—the only language the average prospect understands at all," he said. "How foolish to believe a person merely hearing your salestalk, which bristles perhaps with technical and trade terms, will understand it as well as you, who have been over it 1,000 times."

Try your presentation out on uninformed persons. Kennedy used young people between 14 and 20. He'd repeat his salestalk to them, noting their expressions, questioning if they understood every word.

If he found a cloudy expression, he'd stop right there: he knew he wasn't getting through. Only when his talk sailed along and every person understood did Kennedy know his prospects would.

Does building such a foundation seem like a lot of trouble? It *is*. But it makes sales. What else matters?

Another Kennedy rule: during your talk, before you close, summarize what you have already told the customer. You've said it. He's heard it. Repeat it. Bring your entire talk into focus so there's no misunderstanding anywhere.

All successful communicators, from prophets to trial lawyers, go to great lengths to get complete understanding. They agree with the Apostle Paul in his Epistle to the Corinthians: "I had rather speak five words with understanding than 10,000 words in an unknown tongue."

USE LANGUAGE AS A WEAPON

Experienced closers are almost always expert users of language. Words are your stock in trade—in addition to your real product, of course. When you know and draw on a varied inventory of language, you're way out in front of other sales-people who won't take the trouble to collect and polish words. Two examples show how this works.

1. In the 1950s, Eisenhower delegates to the national Republican convention were challenging the seating of Taft delegates. Herb Brownell, Ike's astute manager, introduced an amendment to the rules which set Ike's people well ahead. He labeled it The Fair Play Amendment. This reduced Taft supporters to speaking against "the so-called Fair Play Amendment." You do not have to be a political buff to know they were licked before they started. Taft never made it to the White House.

Brownell, of course, went on to become Ike's attorney general. This brilliant lawyer could have been a crackerjack salesman as well.

2. James Webb Young, a master mass salesman, retired to New Mexico and set about selling apples grown on his own ranch. He sold Uncle Jim's apples by mail as business gifts for Christmas.

One fall, disaster struck. Just before picking time, a hailstorm hit Jim's orchards, putting small pockmarks in otherwise perfect fruit. At first Jim thought of returning the money to his customers. Then inspiration hit him. With each bushel he sent this note: "You might see some small pockmarks on my apples this year. They're hail marks. They won't hurt the flavor or texture. They're your proof that these delicious apples were grown up here in the high mountain country of New Mexico where the air and soil are just about as perfect as you can find for apple growing."

Not one customer asked for a refund. In fact, for the next couple of years customers wrote to ask if Jim could send them genuine hail-marked apples!

CHECK FOR CLARITY

Make sure the customer understands everything. Ask:

- "Have I made everything clear to you so far, Mr. Robinson?"
- "Is there any other information I can give you, Mrs. Carroll?"

If you get assurance the prospect understands everything, move ahead. But don't be too sure even then. Keep fishing for admissions that indicate some phase of your explanation hasn't been made thoroughly clear.

Don't try to close until you're sure the prospect *does* understand.

Summarize your advantage points in an abundantly clear short sentence. That great mass salesman, Theodore F. Mac-Manus, was responsible for selling hundreds of millions of dollars' worth of automobiles. MacManus wants you to take this test: "Can you summarize the advantages to your prospect in one short, simple, crystal-clear, convincing sentence? When you can do this, you have a background for closing more sales."

Like doctors, salespeople may bury their mistakes—in monthly or weekly averages. But mail-order advertising is either a success or failure on the record. Look at famous money-making ad headlines that have consistently sold products and services over the years. It's a useful exercise in stating benefits in one sentence:

- The secret of making people like you
- A little mistake that cost a farmer $3000 a year
- How a new discovery makes a plain girl beautiful
- Do you make these mistakes in English?
- Who ever heard of a woman losing weight—and enjoying three delicious meals at the same time?
- Another woman is waiting for every man—and she's too smart to have "morning mouth"
- They laughed when I sat down at the piano—but not when I started to play!
- No more back-breaking garden chores for ME—yet ours is now the showplace of the neighborhood!
- Imagine me—holding an audience spellbound for 30 minutes!
- It's a shame for you not to make good money—when these men do it so easily
- A wonderful two years' trip with full pay—but only those with imagination can take it
- Former barber earns $8000 in four months as real estate specialist

Can you summarize your product or service benefit in a sentence as dramatic and as compelling? If not, better start working on it. Dramatic benefit sentences close sales.

Make sure you tell a complete story to every prospect and customer. Here's where many salespeople fail—they simply don't make the prospect understand the basic advantages of buying. It's so easy for you, living with the presentation and giving it 20 times a day, to acquire contempt for some of the simple things you tell customers.

"Anybody can see this product will do such and such a thing," you say. "Why insult the intelligence of the customers by repeating such simple stuff?"

So little by little you drop out essential information. You understand it and therefore conclude your customers understand it. This is a fatal error. You must stick to basics. You must summarize. Measure your presentation against this closing wrap-up:

"Now, Mr. Britten, I know you realize from statements I've already made that this product will save you a considerable amount of money, conserve a great deal of your time, and eliminate much unnecessary work. I've proved what it has done for many other users. The facts and figures I've cited prove no expense has been spared in assuring the quality of this product is what you would naturally expect from a well-known firm like ours.

"But I'd also like you to picture in your own mind why it's so important for you to enjoy immediately the advantages of this product. Surely the saving of $1000 dollars a year means as much to you as it does to those companies I've mentioned.

"Of course, saving an hour a day is probably even more worthwhile to you because of your busy schedule. I'm sure you have many productive things to do with the extra time each day. That is why it's very much to your advantage to accept this opportunity at once. Another reason why immediate action is attractive: at present our company is offering a special discount...."

If you're not being that basic in your closing summation, you're not being fundamental enough to become a champion closer.

WHY PLANNED TALK IS BEST

Organized salestalk is more effective than sporadic talk. Such salestalk must be worked out beforehand, rehearsed, and practiced until it includes everything the prospect needs to know. When you tell a complete story, closing the sale becomes a perfectly natural and almost automatic last step. Hard closing is usually unnecessary if the prospect thoroughly understands.

Theodore M. Bernstein, the watch-your-language editor of *The New York Times*, admonished writers: "It's not enough to make sure you are understood. You must make absolutely certain you cannot be *mis*understood."

Better advice for language of closing sales doesn't exist.

ESTABLISH BELIEF

Equally important is establishing absolute belief.

No sale can be satisfactorily closed without belief. You'll find rules for establishing belief in Chapter 4, in particular the interesting transformation that takes place in the buyer's mind at the moment of buying. The fundamentals of establishing belief are not this book's assignment. At any event, be aware that the *conviction* step comes before the *closing* step.

CREATE WANT

The third brass-tack essential: create desire in the customer's mind. This step, too, must be taken before you reach closing. Wants are created by appealing to motives which cause people to buy what you are selling.

The chief motivations to buying are your prospect's desire for:

- Health, for wealth, for admiration of others (good old-fashioned vanity in action)
- The gratification of some appetite
- The opportunity for amusement (which sells golf clubs, travel service, and the like)
- The safety and security of self and family (which is also called self-improvement)

- Utility or use value of product or service being sold

In addition, one of the most effective sale closers is weakness. To become a closing specialist, always remember buyer weakness.

We all have it. We cannot say no when a gracious, insistent, and dynamic salesperson gives us good reason to buy.

Possibly four out of five sales are closed because the salesperson appeals strongly and correctly to the buyer weakness. (More about this in Chapter 6.)

THE CARNY PUSH

In your own selling experience, you've probably had buyers on the verge of signing many times—but you didn't know it. They were ready for the close. If you'd had the courage to push, they'd have given you the order. But you let up a little on the selling pressure and they escaped.

A little more persuasion on your part, a little more drive, a little more insistence, a little more pressure, and you'd have closed many of those sales then and there. It's human to yield to buyer weakness. Only a very strong-willed customer can resist the gentle but strong persuasion of a salesperson who knows the product and knows how to close.

Charlie Bigelow, a great salesman and as strong a closer as ever existed, learned a valuable secret from traveling carnivals. You know how persuasive the barkers are, how alluringly they depict attractions just on the other side of the canvas.

"I often wondered," said Bigelow, "why—when the barker finished his pitch—it was *easier* to go up to the window and pay than to back out. I felt caught in an irresistible tide that seemed to come from behind. I might be wavering in indecision. But invariably, if I listened to the barker I'd go to his show— whether it interested me or not.

"Later, I found out why. That surge that carried me forward wasn't spontaneous at all. It was engineered. In the back of the crowd were *pushers*—people assigned to push the crowd toward the ticket seller. They shoved you gently forward at the right moment. You didn't know this, of course. You yielded. You moved closer. You bought. That was superb salesmanship, based on the weakness in each of us. We're unable to resist the right kind of push at the moment of buying."

Does Bigelow use the same pusher tactics in closing?

"I don't go around physically pushing my prospects," said he. "But I use the same principle exactly. Realizing it's difficult for a prospect to say *no* to a salesperson who pushes hard for an order, and recognizing the weakness in each of us, I try to close every sale. Not the browbeating tactics of the old-time high-pressure artist. I'm subtle, gracious—but insistent. And it seems to work."

GOOD CLOSERS TRY ONCE MORE

Every customer has this element of weakness in his or her makeup. Each can be closed if you have the courage to try once more. This is sufficient reason to keep on going when the customer tells you he's not going to buy.

Learn this one principle and remember it always: the buyer's no doesn't always mean the buyer cannot be sold. It may mean the buyer needs pressure that appeals to weakness—the gentle pushing that's almost irresistible, if properly applied at the proper time. Each salesperson worth his or her salt keeps on trying to close the sale long after the customer has announced: "I'm not going to buy."

That's another secret of great closers: they always try one more time to close the sale.

DEVELOP
YOUR CLOSING
CONSCIOUSNESS

3

PHYSICALLY, Rocky Bleier was dealt a bad run of cards. He was severely wounded by shrapnel in Vietnam. Doctors said he'd never walk again. Yet he was determined not only to walk but to *play football*.

Bleier was determined. He never stopped trying. He never stopped thinking about playing football.

He played halfback for the Pittsburgh Steelers for ten years and he was a big factor on the only team to win four Super Bowls.

Rocky grabbed at every chance. He ran while other backs stood still.

"The instant before I see light I run," he said.

This same success consciousness is present among great closers. The minute they see light, the slightest chance to succeed, they start throwing closing action at the prospect.

While other salespeople are standing on one foot waiting for the prospect to make up his or her mind, champions are in there closing, closing, closing.

OVERALL CLOSING AWARENESS

George N. Kahn,* a Connecticut marketing consultant, believes the salesperson must have a close-the-sale awareness in every waking moment. It takes time to develop this, of course, but it pays off big.

Says Kahn:

> Closing a sale is like the approach of a shy suitor.
>
> He wants to marry his girl and she is more than ready to accept. But he cannot bring himself to pop the question and chatters on about irrelevant matters.
>
> The woman in the example can steer the conversation back on the main track. A prospect, however, usually offers no such help and often the order is lost because the salesperson simply doesn't know how to close.
>
> Even while a buyer is offering objections, he or she may well be psychologically ready to give you an order. All the buyer needs is assurance from you that he or she is making the right decision.
>
> The buyer has doubts, fears, and apprehensions like anyone else. You must direct his or her thinking into proper buying channels. How? By always being on the offensive. Always think close-the-sale. Beat back objections with strong counter arguments until the prospect has exhausted the reasons for not buying. Then move in quickly and close.

Objections are excuses. No professional should be discouraged by a prospect who says he's:

- bound up with other producers.
- buying from too many different firms now.
- reducing his inventory.
- waiting until business conditions pick up.
- using a product like yours.

Turn these negatives into positives with your agile mind and strong belief in superiority of your product.

---

*See Acknowledgments at front of book.

When to close? Some veterans claim there is only one psychological moment. One-chance closing may occur once in 20 interviews. The other 19 offer several opportunities for closing. Always seize your opportunity.

There is nothing wrong in using a little pressure. Often it works. Many prospects, bored by the soft sell, welcome a push. Help them make up their minds. Buyers often toss in objections, not out of conviction, but as a means of obscuring their own doubts and indecision. They're on the fence and waiting for you to knock them off.

Prospect: "I don't think I'm ready to buy right now."

You: "Mr. Smith, I think you're as ready as you'll ever be. If there is still something you're in doubt about, name it and I'll clear it up. Otherwise, why don't we get on with it?"

Prospect: "Your company is a little high in price."

You: "If that's all that's worrying you, you may as well sign right now. Our prices are competitive. You won't do better anywhere in the industry."

Telling lies to close never pays. Don't say prices are going up if they're not. Don't say your product's raw material is in short supply if it isn't. These tactics will invariably boomerang.

Make a list of stock objections so you can counter them and close more sales in less time.

Selling is a game of chess. The more often you counter your opponent's move, the quicker your victory.

Don't sidestep a serious objection. Meet it squarely. But once you answer it, don't belabor the point. Give the buyer a chance to buy.

CLOSING CONSCIOUSNESS

You simply must have closing consciousness to become a great salesperson. Closing awareness rests, of course, upon alertness.

George Handler, a great salesman, consciously exercised day after day to develop alertness.

"A salesperson has to think fast and act fast," he said. "I was once a slow thinker. My reflexes were not developed like a featherweight boxer's—the way they are now. So I had to force myself to be alert and to catch signs."

He discovered a close relationship between physical and mental alertness. For weeks he practiced sitting in a chair, standing up swiftly—then bounding up, until his muscles were on edge with alertness.

Then Handler carried the development into the mind. He began paying rapt attention to what everyone was saying, listening to exact shadings of words.

Handler was ahead of his time. Today, expensive alertness seminars attract salesfolk and executives—formal training in alertness. You can also do it yourself, as George Handler did.

CREATE CHANCES AS YOU GO

By training yourself in alertness, you create closing chances as you go along. Your prospect may not be aware of these opportunities, but that doesn't matter. You will be.

A sale is merely a series of opportunities to close. A good salesperson seizes them. A poor salesperson muffs them, or, worse, is unaware that they exist.

Buyers, if you are alert, will tell you when they're ready to buy. Not in so many words, but by actions. They finger your sample. They tap the table. They lean forward.

If they open their eyes wider, it's almost certain they want to know more.

Buyers may show they're ready by finding fault with your product. Good salesmen close on resistance. When buyers say they aren't going to buy, take it as a sign—they will.

Usually buyers aren't conscious of giving themselves away. History gives us an illustration.

Gene Tunney, perhaps the craftiest boxer who ever lived, knocked out Tom Gibbons. Yet Gibbons, a marvelous defensive fighter, was flawless. Jack Dempsey hadn't been able to knock him out in 15 rounds. No one could touch Gibbons. Yet, Tunney knocked Gibbons out with a punch to the liver.

Earlier, Tunney had noticed that just before Gibbons threw a punch, he momentarily left his liver unguarded. Tunney watched for the sign. It showed. Whammy—down went Gibbons.

"Tommy never knew he had this weakness," said Tunney later. "But I studied his pictures. I knew it. So I took advantage of it."

The modern salesperson operates this way all the time.

CLOSE EARLIER AND MORE

Hugh Bell closed more by closing twice as early. His record proved him right.

When Hugh was young and inexperienced (and a stranger in town besides) he wasn't making the grade and other salespeople were. In despair, he attended a sales rally.

"If you don't start to close twice as early," the speaker said, "you won't have a chance to close at all."

Afterwards, Hugh Bell asked the speaker to explain.

"Train yourself to close twice as early," the old hand said. "Tomorrow, long before you think you are ready to close, try to close anyway."

"I tried it the next day," Hugh said, "and closed two sales I would have missed if I had held back. Ever since then I've tried to close twice as soon. Believe me it works."

Develop your closing consciousness. Try early. Don't be afraid to be turned down.

CLOSING MOMENTUM

A top Philadelphia salesman demonstrates another way to develop closing consciousness. He had prospects of all shapes and sizes. Yet surprisingly he usually picked a *small* prospect for the first presentation of the day. Why not work on the big ones when you are rested and fresh?

"The quicker you launch yourself into sales, the better you are all day," he said. "I try for an immediate sale on my first call. The amount isn't important. The sale is. With that sale on my order blank, I'm building momentum.

"By midafternoon, I am at my best. I'm self-assured and feeling powerful. My order book is full of sales. I'm loaded for bear."

Ben Sweeney, who sold houses, used showmanship to develop his closing consciousness. In showing a house,

Sweeney always unearthed a rusty old horseshoe somewhere on the premises. He casually showed it to the prospect but didn't emphasize it. The prospect's mind was thinking: "Good luck." Usually, without any help from Sweeney, the prospect would decide on the house.

Another salesman, selling fire extinguishers, set his own car on fire. (He had previously poured a small quantity of gasoline on the block.) After putting out the fire, he said to the prospect: "Lucky I had one of these extinguishers with me. Saved a $5,000 car." You know the rest.

WHAT CLOSING CONSCIOUSNESS IS NOT

Since you're learning what closing consciousness is, it's important to know what it *isn't—simplistic enthusiasm.* Samuel S. Susser, a 40-year-sales veteran with Ethyl Corporation, says you do not need to "bubble with enthusiasm even on your bad days, and immediately after (if not during) funerals, floods, and disasters.

"You are told that if you do not radiate bubbling enthusiasm you will not be able to sell," Susser says. "That a buyer will immediately buy or not buy in ratio to the hot glow he feels or does not feel oozing out of your eyeballs into his. This presumes the buyer is stupid and that high on his criteria for a purchasing determination is the salesperson's childish enthusiasm.

"An intelligent buyer, even one of low I.Q., is ofter scared to death of an aggressive enthusiastic seller. Are some products sold that way? Yes, but only to the most unsophisticated consumer of used cars, home repairs, and insurance policies. Never to a professional buyer."

How come in movies, some toothy enthusiast invariably selects *enthusiasm* as the single most desirable asset in a salesperson? On your next call, pour it on like you see in the movies, Susser says. If he likes you, he may say: "Look, Joe, I've been buying from you because you were a nice guy to talk to about my problems. You could always answer my questions about the product, and you never gave me this high-powered selling.

"So what's happened to you—you feeling all right? You always sold me like a pro. Now all of a sudden you're acting like some of these kids I throw out of here twice a day."

Don't try overenthusiasm on an experienced buyer. Susser says, "It could cost you."

DRAW FROM ACES

Another way to develop closing consciousness is to pattern yourself on a success.

W. Clement Stone, wealthy Chicago insurance tycoon and one of the nation's famous salesmen, put it bluntly: "If you want success, copy from success.

"We all need a model. If we select the right model, nothing can be of more help. The trouble is many of us follow false models.

"Discover the most successful salesman in your line, the strongest closer. Then discover, if you can, the reason for his success. If you look long enough you can find it. When you find the reasons for success, relate his techniques to your life, and success is easy."

Don't ape anyone, Stone made clear. You can learn his principles and adapt them to your personality.

Frank H. Davis, one of the world's greatest insurance salesmen, imparted his closing principles to everyone who worked for him. They wanted to close like the old man. Vast numbers did.

Bill Goebel, one of Davis' greatest admirers, asked himself during his presentations: "What would Frank do? How would he get the sale?"

Learn in your formative years to imitate closing methods of a great salesman. It will advance your success considerably.

DON'T FOLLOW THE LEADER

In developing a constant orientation toward closing—as you must—the tried-and-true path isn't always the answer. Get out and cut some new trails, Joe Gary says.

Gary, marketing vice-president of AECO Products Division, National Services Industries, Atlanta, is himself a crackerjack personal salesman. Says Gary:

> Some salespeople achieve more because they're *not* following the leader. Innovators uncover hidden problems and offer sound solutions. They practice investigative selling.
> You don't become an innovator by chance. Make a conscious effort to sell in depth. Stop trying to get the same order everyone else is after. Go for the creative sale, not the commodity.
> The greater the challenge, the greater the reward.
> An envelope's an envelope, right? Not hardly. Our customer was using a vinyl envelope with three pockets. The envelope, stored in a file folder, was printed in white on an orange background.
> Some salesmen would have said: "That's that!" Our salesman did not. He recommended an envelope made of Polywove, a very strong lightweight material. He recommended two connected envelopes with an index tab on one side.
> The buyer liked it. A cost analysis indicated enormous savings.
> The salesman presented in detail to the department using the envelope. He wrote a very large order.
> He learned the customer's business. He isolated a product he could replace. He conceptualized a product and prepared a prototype.
> The sale developed in well-prepared natural sequence. Our salesman got approval at each stage before moving to the next.
> Build a profile of each customer's needs. Revise it constantly. Each customer call is a learning experience.
> You can develop selling skills, build great prospect lists, work territory efficiently, offer salable products competitively priced, and *still not* reach true potential—unless you realize your product must satisfy customer needs.
> Uncover and develop that need. There's more to closing sales than showing wares.

Joe Gary's salesman has closing awareness. His record proves it.

AUTOCONDITIONING

Autoconditioning is another way of developing closing consciousness.

You condition your mind to do almost anything you want it to—from mastering a new subject to making you alert to opportunities around you. Here's how it works.

1. *Define what you want.* You want to develop closing consciousness, of course.
2. *Live with the idea.* Think about closing, closing opportunities, closing keys, closing, closing, closing, all the time.
3. *Wait for the breakthrough.* You will gradually develop the alertness you seek.

Soon you'll be perceiving closing opportunities you're not aware of now. You'll learn how to detect signs you didn't know existed. Your mind will be conditioned to make the most of every prospect.

Give yourself a cross-exam each night. Carry prospect cards home. Go over your calls. Did certain prospects show signs you didn't perceive at the time? What did the prospect say that should have led you to try to close? How many chances did you muff because you weren't alert?

A salesperson with proper closing consciousness is like a lively thoroughbred at the starting gate. Everything is tuned to get out in front.

That soon will be you. Think, live, and act *closing* each hour of the day. Soon closing will be part of your *persona* and part of your life.

LEARN TO CLOSE FIRST IN YOUR OWN MIND

4

"CLOSING," the crackerjack salesman exclaimed, "is the easiest part of the sale. Many salesmen make hard work of it and fear it. But that's because their concept of closing is not right. They try to close sales in the prospect's mind, which means struggle. My plan is much simpler. I close the sale in my own mind. Then the actual closing is easy."

This had been his approach ever since, as a sprouting salesman, he had gone to work with an old hand, the experienced salesman, who made good records but never seemed to be in a hurry.

The young salesman was full of vinegar. He wanted to get everything done right away. He raced from call to call and tried to rush buyers off their feet. He gave every prospect the works, but it didn't pay off and he was getting nothing for his efforts but spinning wheels. The old-timer took him in hand.

"Take it easier," he admonished. "You're *preventing* sales with your aggressive attitude. You are talking to people twice your age. These mature people need to be led. No one can drive them, not even their spouses. So what chance have you?"

The older salesman then advised the apprentice to make a sale first in his own mind.

"See yourself signing the order," he said. "Know you are going to win. Then when you are with the prospect you can act at ease and be patient. Since you can't force him, let him take his time. Hang loose.

"You will find it easy to sell a prospect if you make the sale to yourself first."

The more the salesman thought about it, the more right it seemed. Then he dug in and found psychological reason why it works.

SELL YOURSELF FIRST

Through a strange alchemy of mind which no one quite understands (yet every scientist recognizes) we transmit our thoughts, our feelings, our expectations, our exultations, our fears, and our doubts to people we talk to. They transmit *their* thoughts, feelings, expectations, exultations, fears, and doubts to *us*. We sense these emotions. We do not know why or how. Many explanations have been given, from thought transference to ESP.

If you don't know how these transmissions are made, at least recognize they *are* made. That knowledge becomes equipment for a good closer.

One of the greatest sales managers America has ever known—George Hopkins—believed so heartily in closing consciousness that he told his salespeople each day when they started out: "Remember one thing—*expect* success. Expect success from morning till night, and you will get it. If you expect failure, failure will come to you just as surely as day follows night."

Hopkins insisted that his salespeople go through a little ritual each time they made a sales call. The salesperson had to tell himself: "I am going to sell this man. I know I am."

Naturally, Hopkins' salespeople were not successful in selling every buyer. Who is? But by learning to expect success they failed in far fewer cases than if their attitude had been doubt or defeat.

In Baltimore, the rich and respected president of an international business believes this rule goes far deeper than closing sales. It embraces an entire working philosophy of life. He describes it as "thinking lucky."

This hasn't always been easy. He struggled for years to get a foothold as a salesman. Ill health dogged him. He kept thinking lucky. His best-laid plans went haywire. He kept thinking lucky. His best customers failed him, as they do occasionally with every salesperson. No matter what happened, he continually kept thinking lucky.

This salesman believes his success today has come from always thinking lucky. Everywhere he carries the attitude and bearing of a man who knows he's going to win. This man practiced—throughout his sales life—the one fundamental that will enable any salesperson to sell more:

"Develop the attitude that you cannot fail. Insist on the positive expectation of success."

If you have that, you have everything. If you lack that, you lack everything. Development of this positive expectation in closing sales does two important things for you:

1. It gives you the pleasing attitude and bearing of self-confidence to establish conviction. In closing sales, you must have self-confidence.

2. It transmits your assurance in yourself to your customer—in the mysterious way we don't understand but which we applaud nonetheless. The customer is thereby influenced to do what you want him to do.

This book gives you many definite and tangible closing techniques. But they all depend upon this cornerstone: you must communicate, in everything you do, that you can and will close every sale.

When you talk to your customer, assume he or she is going to buy, that he or she can't help buying from you. Express it in the way you talk, the words you choose. If you are positive in your own mind that the customer will buy, this positiveness will be apparent when you talk. Your attitude will say the customer is going to buy, there is no doubt about it. The only question is when and how much!

It's difficult for you to develop and maintain this positive attitude at first. That's natural enough. Probably before you call upon a buyer, you decide that he or she is the kind you cannot sell. Another, you decide, hasn't enough money. Running through your mind are unwelcome thoughts that you do not have what it takes to become a great salesperson.

DUMP NEGATIVE BAGGAGE NOW

There's only one way to overcome negative slants on life (and I view this not as a quack psychologist but as a hard-boiled pragmatist who's seen 50,000 salespeople in action). The only way to banish these negatives from your selling life is to do just that—get rid of them right now, before they increase.

If you question your ability, if you wonder if you're cut out for selling, don't let these notions get a foothold.

"Ah," you say, "but how?"

Well, be bold. Drive them from your mind. Put them out of your life. Put them out for good. In their place, plant the idea you can sell as well as any other person alive, that the next prospect you call upon is as good as sold already.

There's nothing more important in your entire selling life than your attitude toward your ability to close.

Don't, of course, say to yourself: "I am a closing genius. No one can resist me. I am indomitable," and expect to be transformed into a master salesperson. The closing attitude needs more substantial nourishment than mere dreams. It needs to feed on facts. And the facts are easily available.

According to Gustave Le Bon, the greatest of crowd psychologists, nothing can touch a practice called *affirmation*. You can start using it right away.

When you *affirm*, you repeat a word or phrase over and over until it becomes etched in your subconscious mind.

As a means of controlling your own mind (making yourself do and believe the things you want to do and believe) nothing can touch *affirmation*. If you affirm a thing often enough, it controls your own mind.

Affirmation works miracles. Here's how. Let us say that you recognize that negative feelings are holding you back—that optimists achieve and pessimists fail. How can you affirm yourself into a positive frame of mind? Just do it. Say to yourself:

"I *really* enjoy being myself. I really enjoy being happy and succeeding."

Take it on the authority of the greatest psychologists: if you repeat what you want to believe often enough it *will* come to pass. This is not a new idea. It's a greatly *unused* classic idea.

AVOID NAY-SAYERS

To banish negative thoughts in selling, your most important step is avoiding nay-sayers. Don't associate with negative people. O.C. Halyard, dynamic training vice-president of Real Estate One, in Maitland, Florida, tells his sales trainees:

> You must learn to overcome fear. We all have fears, some realistic—some not; fear of failure, fear of being a failure, fear of being rejected. Rejection comes in the form of a No. You tend to take a No as a personal rejection. It hurts the ego.
>
> Consequently, people avoid giving others opportunity to reject them. Unfortunately, when you fail to provide opportunities for a No, you also eliminate opportunities to get a Yes.
>
> The person who rejects your services today may accept what you offer tomorrow. People are impressed by perseverance. They recall you as a hard worker who will go all the way for them.
>
> Avoid negative persons. They rehash the deal that fell through or grouse that somebody else gets all the good prospects. Tell such people you'd like to talk, but have work to do. Don't become their wailing wall—lest you emerge with a negative feeling yourself. Think and work positively to be successful.

KNOWLEDGE IS POWER

To provide yourself with a solid base of confidence, you must:

1. Acquire knowledge, full knowledge, complete knowledge, of your product or the service—knowledge of what it is, how it is made, what it will do, what it will mean to your customer. Such knowledge you simply must possess.

2. Arm yourself with knowledge of your customer, complete knowledge of his needs and his desires. You must know almost as much about him as he knows about himself.

3. Anticipate every objection that might possibly arise during the interview and be prepared to answer it.

4. Know yourself. Know your strong points (we all have them) and your weak points (we all have them, too, alas). Remember the sage advice of Socrates: "Know thyself." And, later, remember the counsel of Scottish poet Robert Burns: "Oh wad some power the gifti gie us/To see oursels as others see us!"

Check up on yourself regularly to see whether you are improving or retrogressing. Knowing yourself is important. Some salesfolk believe nothing else matters as much in becoming a good closer.

MARY KAY'S POSITIVE THINKING

Mary Kay Ash is chairman of Mary Kay Cosmetics, Inc., a Dallas-based direct-to-consumer selling company. Her company reports more than $200 million in sales each year. Mary Kay's entire career is a tribute to her positive thinking, her knowledge of herself, and her sense of humor about herself.

She hates to see human potential undeveloped.

"In every group, there are (1) people who make things happen, (2) those who watch things happen, (3) people who wonder what happened, and (4) those who don't know anything happened," Mary Kay says. "Many of us die with our music unplayed. My mother, who worked from 6 a.m. to 8 p.m. to support us, always said: 'Honey, you can do *any*thing in this world you want to do.' The adage became part of my life."

Many years ago, Mary Kay needed a job that allowed her to support three children and still be home part of the time. She started selling Stanley Products on the home party plan.

"At the end of my third week, I was averaging $7.00 in sales per home party," she relates. "At that time we gave away a complimentary $4.99 mop and duster when we entered the hostess' door. So you can see I was operating dreadfully in the red."

Mary Kay heard about a Stanley sales convention in Dallas. She borrowed the money to attend.

"I converted my sample case to a suitcase," she recalls. "I took along a box of crackers and a pound of cheese; I had no extra money for food. I also put on a hat people had laughed at for 10 years."

On the train to Dallas, the women sang Stanley songs. Mary Kay was embarrassed. She pretended she wasn't part of the group.

At the hotel when the other women decided to go out for dinner, she'd say: "Excuse me, there's something I need to do in my room." She'd go and eat cheese and crackers.

At that convention, she watched them crown a saleswoman Queen and give her an alligator bag. She decided on the spot that's where she wanted to be next year.

She marched up to Stanley Beveridge, the company president, and said:

"Mr. Beveridge, next year I am going to be Queen."

He looked her straight in the eye and said: "Somehow I think you will."

The next year she *was* Queen.

"You need the right mental attitude," Mary Kay says. "If you think you can, you can. If you think you can't, you're right. I know it's an old idea but it's great.

"If you act enthusiastic, you will become enthusiastic. At first maybe you fake it—but then, it happens."

The bumble bee's body, according to aerodynamics, is too heavy to fly, she relates. The wings are too weak. But the bumble bee doesn't know it and goes right on flying.

"What a wonderful symbol for salespeople who don't know they can fly and who do," she says.

Everyone must develop a goal. Each of us possesses infinitely more talent than we ever use, she believes.

"Whatever you vividly imagine, ardently desire, sincerely believe and enthusiastically act on must inevitably come to pass," she says.

"When you want to do something, and you don't know

how, start anyhow—and the pieces fall into place." Mary Kay believes good closers are activists. She reminds you:

"On the plains of hesitation bleach the bones of countless thousands who, on the threshold of victory, hesitated and, while hesitating, died."

CHECK UP ON YOURSELF

The sales manager of an international company recently said: "I didn't begin to make much headway until I started checking up on myself. By that I mean a systematic method of finding out whether I was going ahead or backward in my sales contacts."

How did he do this?

"I used John D. Rockefeller's system," he responded. "Every night before he dropped off to sleep, Rockefeller spent ten minutes reviewing the day. He tried to find reasons for successes. He was even more analytical about his failures."

The sales manager converted this system to sales calls.

"The last ten minutes of every day I go over everything that has happened," he said. "I am mercilessly truthful. If I have made an ass of myself in an interview, I don't try to find an excuse for it. I call myself an ass—and decide to be a higher-type animal in the future.

"With sales contacts that have been successful, I ask: why? I look for the answer. When I've been unsuccessful, I ask: why?

"In 90 days, after I began getting better acquainted with myself, I had lifted myself from a failure to success in selling."

What do you look for in these personal checkups? Balance. *Self-confidence*, for example, is a valuable—even necessary—trait in selling. But too much confidence is a detriment, not a help, for it will become *arrogance* or *conceit*—sure death to sales.

Too much confidence could make you argumentative, so positive you're right that you win arguments and lose sales—win battles and lose wars.

That's why you need regular self-analysis. Keep on a moderate course of gentle positiveness that rests on factual confidence. Aristotle had a name for this right closing attitude.

He called it The Golden Mean. Successful closers call it The Professional Attitude.

There's a communications system between salesperson and prospect that tells the prospect you *know* you can sell him. It's built on your personal appearance, your manner, and your feeling toward the prospect.

A brilliant young salesperson of business properties in Chicago describes it this way:

"Your appearance says things about you before you even open your mouth. In my continual survey of real estate people, I find a direct correlation between the salesperson's success and appearance.

"Appearance not only has an effect upon the client or prospect, but also upon the salesperson.

"You cannot make a strong close while wearing a dirty shirt or blouse!"

TALK SUCCESS

Your speech is part of your appearance. Keep your talk pleasant. Be cheerful—deliver good news! Create a positive climate on which people can depend.

Don't be overanxious. You are not anxious to close a deal, so don't talk like it. You are the prospect's able, knowledgeable, professional counsel. You are retained by him or her to handle the technical, financial, and legal aspects of a transaction.

Know your voice. You sound differently to others than to yourself. A tape recorder will prove it. A monotonous tone with words spaced like pickets in a fence will lose attention.

Watch the last word of each sentence. Keep it up. One of Los Angeles' most successful salesmen has been practicing voice exercises for years. He tapes his own voice, listens critically to the playback, and works at developing a clear, interesting voice. It pays him very well.

Your speech is part of your appearance. Is yours up to snuff?

BERT SCHLAIN'S FORMULA

Bert Schlain believes that *lack of worry* is a great contributor to closing in your own mind. Bert's been practicing it for 60 years as salesman, sales manager, and consultant. Here's his prescription:

"Put each day into a capsule and use that day to the fullest. Yesterday is a canceled check. Tomorrow is a promissory note. Today is cash—the only life we have to live.

"Tension, anger, hatred, and hair-trigger temper bring on high blood pressure and lead to indigestion, ulcers, heart attack, stroke. Avoid such debilitating emotions."

Eat, drink, and be merry—sensibly and moderately, Bert believes. If you must drink, set a sensible limit and stick to it.

"About beer: a little is a tonic. Too much is Teutonic," he says. "Get to bed in a serene frame of mind. If you read in bed, eschew action-filled books or suspenseful mysteries. Stick to travel, philosophy, history—restful and calming subjects.

"Don't borrow trouble. Many anticipated troubles never happen. Do today's tasks today—starting with the most urgent and working down. Sufficient unto the day is the evil thereof."

You can be old at 30 and young at 80, Bert Schlain says.

"If you look forward to learning and doing new things, visiting new places, meeting new people, enjoying new experiences, testing new amusements, you're young!

"Pointless, aimless worrying accomplishes nothing. It can only worsen your mental and emotional state.

"Enjoy making others happy. Enjoy living every moment of every day. Relegate sad events to the pages of your memory book. Continue doing, planning, achieving, enjoying!"

Another sage counselor, Leroy (Satchel) Paige, said it this way:

"Take it easy on the vices. The social ramble ain't restful. Don't eat fried foods. They angrify the blood. Don't look back. Something may be gaining on you."

Either way, self-knowledge and self-management are the keys to closing sales in your own mind first of all. You control yourself because you know yourself.

In fact, this is the attitude of the well-trained man or woman in any field—doctor, lawyer, dentist, nurse. This is the serene, superlatively poised attitude that says you know you are right and don't have to go around proving it. This is the attitude that will help you close more sales.

But no sale is one-sided. Two persons are involved. You are one-half. The customer is the other half. His or her role is equally important, naturally enough.

So we'll also look inside the customer's mind at the time when closing occurs. Then you'll see how to make this positive expectation of yours dovetail with the peculiarities of the customer.

TURN YOURSELF INTO A POWERFUL CLOSER

5

BECOMING a powerful closer is an attainable goal. I tell you how to do it and give you directions for becoming a powerful closer whenever you wish to be.

Let's start with a true story of two salespeople. I knew them both on their first selling job. Each appeared equally capable of succeeding.

One of the bright young salespeople always seemed to get the breaks. He closed sales right and left and brought in orders. The other salesperson brought in alibis.

One became the top salesperson for the firm, the big earner, while the other barely got by. Eventually the second man drifted out of selling and I lost track of him. The first man is now sales vice-president of the firm.

What was his secret?

It's very simple. He had *go-ahead*. Whenever he tackled a prospect he went all-out. Some of his ideas were not sound, but his good ideas offset the bad. At year end, his sales were always growing.

Once I accused him of being a born salesman.

"Not at all," said he. "I am always willing to go ahead 95 percent on plans that may not be more that 5 percent right, and the momentum puts me over." This was his candid explanation. I liked it.

During a selling interview, even though conditions were not always right, he went ahead and tried for a close. He didn't wait for ideal conditions.

That's the top secret of developing yourself into a perfect closer—take a chance, go ahead, try for a close.

JOHN CHAPIN'S GO-AHEAD ABILITY

John Chapin sells bicycles. His sales rise 20 percent per year. Once he gets his teeth in a sale, John Chapin will do anything that needs doing to make it work.

"One December, I had pre-sold 22 bicycles as the largest part of Santa's gifts for seven-to-nine-year-old girls," John recalls. "Shipment was delayed by dock and warehouse strikes and then a winter blizzard. On December 21, rather than face 44 parents trying to explain why Santa Claus wasn't coming—and not wanting to lose the sale—I drove 2000 miles round-trip in snow to pick them up."

This above-and-beyond service is a requirement of successful closing. Are you willing to go that far? Ace closers do it.

ASK FOR MORE THAN YOU EXPECT

Frank Irving Fletcher, known for his big fees, said: "A salesman should expect *twice* as much as he gets with the wistful reservation that it's only *half* of what he is worth."

Too many salespeople don't think this way. They want big money but in a timid way. They cannot actually see themselves closing the sales it takes to earn the big money.

One $100,000-a-year salesperson used this formula: "Never be satisfied. Always try to sell every buyer more than he wants. Try to sell more buyers. Be dissatisfied. I am—even now."

T. Coleman Du Pont, of the famous family and firm, gave this advice to salespeople: "Don't be satisfied merely with your share of the business. Want it all. Try to get it all."

DESIRE: KEY TO CLOSING

No man or woman is a native-born poor closer. It's not possible. You may be an *untrained* closer. But if you want to improve your closing ability, you can easily do it.

Desire to do is the key.

Qualities which good closers possess are not spectacular qualities at all. I recollect a giant of a man who weighed some 300 pounds. He had a bluff, hearty, good-natured manner. But he also had considerable drive and as much force as I ever saw in a salesperson. It was practically impossible for an ordinary prospect to deny him. But later his prospects repented at their leisure. His ratio of cancellations was high. So, you see, so-called native abilities can backfire, too.

Today's ace closer has no exclusive attributes out of reach of ordinary salespeople. Indeed, the best closers are quite ordinary in size, in appearance, in demeanor, even in knowledge. But they do have closing ability. The prime characteristic is simply the desire to close more sales.

So simple you might think it hardly worthwhile to list? You'd be astonished at the number of salespeople who are half-hearted about their desire to sell more. Half of your salesforce today, I suspect, are satisfied with far less than they could accomplish, if they'd put more spirit into their work.

GETTING UNDER PROSPECT'S SKIN

Art Harris, manager of retail sales development for WRGB, one of General Electric's stations in Schenectady, NY, believes the best closers get under the prospect's skin. Here are three ways Harris uses this technique to sell television time:

- *Capitalize on interruptions.* Interruptions in sales presentations can provide clues about a prospect.

"My initial visit with Mr. R. was brief and not encouraging," Harris says. "Yet, during my ten minutes in his office, while he took several phone calls, I looked around the room.

"In a glassed-in bookcase, I saw three bound brown-leather copies of Jeppesen's Airway Charts, (I'm an aviation buff.)"

On his way out, Harris asked the receptionist if Mr. R. was interested in aviation. Was he ever! He had his own plane. He expected to get his instrument rating shortly.

Harris sent to Washington for an area aviation chart—fields, airways, omni stations.

The station artist superimposed TV's measured coverage area on this air chart. Harris sent it to Mr. R. The covering letter explained: the station's coverage extends from the Poughkeepsie VOR to the Glens Falls radio beacon—aviation talk, of course.

Harris asked when they could meet again.

"A week later I had a phone call from Mr. R.," Harris says. "Soon I was a passenger in his Piper Twin Comanche. He showed me, in VFR conditions, how his instruments worked."

How could Mr. R. refuse to visit the television station to see new Ampex videotape recorders? Soon Mr. R. was sitting in the control room watching his own TV commercials being taped. Harris had closed the sale.

- *The letter route.* Mr. D. was tougher. He also listened in a perfunctory way. But there were no clues from his office.

Harris gave the parking lot a quick once-over. No clue.

He subscribed to the newspaper in Mr. D.'s city. He struck oil.

"One of the first issues carried a letter from Mr. D.," Harris says. "He protested the proposed razing of an 80-year-old hotel—a historic building that should be preserved."

Harris fired off a letter to Mr. D., agreeing emphatically with his protest. He enclosed a brochure about a historic walking tour of the area.

"Back came the friendliest letter I've ever seen from a prospect," Harris says. "Only three people had commented on his letter. He was astonished that someone so far away had seen it."

Harris closed. Mr. D. became a 52-week buyer for six years.

- *The family: yes and no.*

Get close to the customer. But not ham-handedly. Don't say: "You have a ten-year-old. So do I. Is he in Little League?"

Harris sticks to the prospect himself. He doesn't involve his family *unless* the prospect takes the lead.

"Mr. S. had given me a signed purchase order for TV time," Harris relates. "But he relied on me to pick good spots. As we got better acquainted, we went to the Saratoga racetrack together.

"During business or social hours, Mr. S. never mentioned his family. When he described his forthcoming trip to Japan, I did not ask if his wife was going."

Good thing. Harris later learned Mr. S. had just become a widower. How awkward to come on cornball with, "How's the wife?"

Art Harris learned the value of getting under the customer's skin—with restraint. Closing the sale also means keeping it closed during an on-going relationship.

CLOSING ABOVE ALL ELSE

To great salesfolk, closing sales is the most important thing in the world. They get up out of sick beds, interrupt vacations, and work all night to close sales. One champion salesman told me making a sale meant as much to him as living itself. He was in earnest. To the real dedicated closer, selling *is* living.

Any man or woman who wants to close more sales *can*, provided the desire is in the mind. After that desire is present, certain secondary qualities are often present in the personality and life of great closers:

- *Be positive.* Buyers are often indecisive. If a salesperson is indecisive, that makes it unanimous. Sales (when they occur) are quite accidental. But if a salesperson is positive, he or she can overcome indecision of the buyer and close more sales.

- *Be willing to study buyer needs.* Then translate those needs into services or products. You must look for information that will help the buyer make up his or her mind. Close from the buyer's side of the fence. While this often gives the appearance of low pressure (which is disarming), actually it is salesmanship of the highest order.

- *Respect time.* Only by trading profitably on his or her time does a salesperson make a profitable number of sales. Therefore, rather than wasting time on routine calls or so-called contact calls, effective closers plan their time to spend every possible moment where sales potential is high—not next week, not next month, not even tomorrow, but today.

- *Be persistent.* This quality is almost universal in good closers. Many a salesperson is on the verge of closing an important sale, only to let up just a minute too soon.

   Good closers stay a little bit longer, make one more try, and usually succeed.

- *Evaluate prospects carefully.* Good closers develop a shrewd judgment of just how good a prospect is. They classify prospects as first, second, and third grade. They're not content to spend time on second or third graders when a first grade prospect is around.

- *Tremendous trifles.* Good closers recognize that little things in selling make big differences. That's why they're always trying new closing techniques, why they spend so much time practicing and perfecting methods, and why they are always on the lookout for new opportunities to close more sales.

Don't think good closers are always dynamic, pushing, restless, nervous, greedy. They aren't.

One of the best closers I ever saw gave the impression he was rather reluctant to try to close. But just the same, every word he said, every action he took, was leading to a successful close.

LISTEN EARLY FOR SIGNALS

Warren Armstrong is an advertising agency principal in Lancaster, PA. His job: selling new clients for his firm.

He considers a good ear—that is, listening for buying signals at the first meeting—to be a vital tool in his closing success. Moreover, Armstrong says you must listen *early*.

"Get on base with the prospect in your initial sales call—before the presentation," Armstrong says.

"This means selling yourself and establishing rapport. It means listening. If you don't come away from preliminary meetings with a clear and complete understanding of what the prospect's looking for, you haven't made first base."

Recently Armstrong met with a prestigious retailer. Although founded nearly 200 years ago, this retailer never had an advertising agency. Now he wanted one.

The first two meetings were devoted to listening. As frequently happens, the father and son had different ideas. Armstrong decided to continue meeting until they resolved what they really wanted to accomplish.

"We decided father and son's differing ideas could be settled by marketing research," Armstrong says. "I recommended this. They agreed. Our facts in hand, we presented—not what one or the other wanted—but what research indicated! We got the assignment.

"Listening is the most important tool of all. Talk strategy only after listening instructs you what to say. Closing will succeed only in relation to your ear-analysis power."

KNOWING WHEN NOT TO TALK

Good closers are unerring judges of just how long they should talk. Many salespeople lack this judgment. A salesperson can talk himself into a sale and then talk himself out of it—and often does.

Mark Twain told about a preacher who began exhorting his congregation to give money to send missionaries to China.

The preacher made a masterful presentation. Mark Twain, in the back row, was moved. He resolved to give $25. The preacher went on with his talk. After 15 minutes, Twain cut his contribution down to $10.

The preacher didn't close his sale, but kept on talking. Twain decided to save $5 of his $10 and give only $5.

Still the pastor continued to talk. Twain, more bored, resolved to give only $1. At length, after about another half-hour, the preacher did close. The collection plate was passed. Instead of giving $25 as he had planned in the beginning, Twain took $1 out of the plate!

Good closers realize the fewer words said at the moment of closing, the better. One of the most effective closers, Harry Emsley, had a serious speech impediment. By ordinary standards, he shouldn't have been a salesman at all.

But Harry was a great salesman. He did little talking. Talking was hard on him and harder on the prospect. But he asked questions that led the buyer to conviction. He closed his sales with a minimum of words. More salespeople should take a leaf from that book.

Harry, a beginner, was new to the firm and to the territory. The territory was tough. To send him into that killer territory was like throwing a Christian to the lions. His boss had qualms about ruining such a promising career.

He could have saved his sympathy. Harry Emsley didn't need it. He started making sales. He made larger sales than ever were made in the territory before. He confounded his boss.

He quickly became the number 1 salesman. Why? Harry was an idea man.

He bristled with ideas like a pincushion. He had ideas on how his customers could display products to their best advantage.

"Say, Ed, I was up North last week, and picked up an idea I think you could use here. Let me tell you what it is."

The customers saw themselves cashing in on ideas other retailers had proved out elsewhere.

"If they can do it," they reasoned, "so can I." So they bought ideas from Harry Emsley—and his products.

Harry became a top man. He still goes about his territory with bright new ideas. He's still selling bigger orders.

POWER OF ENTHUSIASM

Another quality present in practically all great closers is priceless *enthusiasm*. Turn them down, repel them, order them out of the office, tell them never to come back, and their enthusiasm is still undiminished. They believe in their company, in their products, in themselves, in their customers, and probably in their stars. They go on in spite of discouragements.

Like the electric fan salesman traveling through northern Alaska calling on Eskimos. As he visited each igloo, the residents would exclaim in amazement: "Fan? What do we want with a fan? It's 60 degrees below zero here now!"

"Sure, I know," soothed the salesman. "But you never can tell about the weather. Tomorrow it may jump up to zero."

KNOWING WHEN TO COOL IT

There are times when the best salespeople change plans and try not for a sale but for an exit. At times, it's good salesmanship *not* to try to close.

Inept salespeople sometimes stick and try to make a sale. Good salespeople leave and come back later when the wind is more favorable.

It takes judgment. It takes more than judgment. It takes *courage* to carry the sale up to a certain point, to cast aside all the advantage you have won, back out, and come back another day. But it's often the best kind of salesmanship. Just as it is often the best military tactic to retreat today and advance tomorrow.

Robert E. Carl, senior vice-president of Vantage Companies, Dallas, learned to retreat today and close tomorrow in selling H. L. Hunt—at that time the richest man in the world.

"Long before his two sons became household names in the silver market, the cherubic-looking Hunt had formed a public affairs organization called Facts Forum," Carl recalls. "Its purpose: to help preserve the free enterprise system through public enlightenment about current political issues."

Carl represented a printing company and had sold Hunt several orders in the past.

The legendary Hunt, a quiet and modest man, shunned publicity. He brought his own lunch to work everyday in a plain paper bag. He drove a three-year-old standard-brand automobile. He wore off-the-rack suits.

"Yet that day the man with a reputed income of $1 million a week was visibly disturbed: not enough people really understood Facts Forum. I saw a selling opportunity."

Carl told H. L. Hunt he'd have a suggestion the next day. His idea: a newsletter.

Back to his own office, he did a layout for *Facts Forum News*, wrote a sample story, estimated printing costs.

"The next day, I presented the plan to Mr. Hunt: low cost versus the broad understanding communicated to thousands throughout the nation," Carl relates. "A falling unit cost as circulation increased."

Hunt listened attentively—and then scowled. He hustled Carl out of his office. Had Carl suggested an overly ambitious idea?

"I wondered through a long weekend where I had gone wrong," Carl said. He had:

Established personal rapport with a qualified buyer.

Demonstrated superiority of product.

Keyed it to the buyer's special problems.

Presented a visual concept of how to meet his needs.

Relegated price to its proper perspective in the decision buying.

Enumerated benefits.

Carl decided not to push and to let Hunt make the next move.

"Monday morning I got a call from Mr. Hunt," Carl says. "He wanted to get started right away! I'd done it right. He was just a slow reactor."

Eventually, *Facts Forum News* became a multi-page national magazine—and a very profitable piece of new business.

"That experience convinced me that—despite cable television, wondrous computers and other sophisticated devices—personal selling will always be a vital and nonreplaceable link in closing sales," Carl says. "Here was a man who could literally buy anything he wanted—but bought only after I personally demonstrated what he really needed."

Bob Carl knew when to effect a strategic retreat. He had to go away and chew nails for a weekend without pressing a good—but easily upset—customer. He closed the sale by knowing *when* to wait.

OTHER CLOSER-KILLERS

Good salespeople also avoid other closer-killers—certain things that kill sales almost invariably, such as:

Overtalking

Giving the appearance of being too eager

Going off half-cocked or making a half-baked presentation

Trying to crowd the buyer too much by poor high-pressure methods

Wandering away from the subject is another effective killer of sales, and so is negativism.

THE PRO AT PRACTICE

It was seven in the morning. The sales counselor, spending time in the field, called on the star salesman.

He heard a voice coming from the salesman's room. He knocked and waited for an invitation to come in.

"I heard you talking," he apologized to the salesman, "and didn't want to interrupt you."

"Oh, I was just rehearsing my sales presentation," said the star salesman.

Later it was seven in the evening. They were going to dinner together.

Again the counselor heard voices inside, so he knocked.

"Oh, no one's here," repeated the salesman. "I am just rehearsing my presentation before dinner."

Did this happen every day?

"Every day," the salesman said, "including Sundays. If I don't rehearse for just one day, my sales suffer."

"How many years have you been selling the same service?"

"For 30 years."

"And you still feel you must rehearse your presentation twice a day?"

"Yes. That is the price of success in selling. Constant rehearsal."

The question to you now is this: are you willing to pay this kind of price to be a champion?

Champion closers are—and do.

After reading these descriptions, you may decide there are many qualities that make a good closer. There are. Even if you do not already have these qualities, you can easily develop many of them. The more you perfect, the more sales you'll close.

YOUR BUYER'S WEAKNESS IS YOUR CLOSING STRENGTH

6

EVERY sale you lose—repeat, *every* sale—will be lost because you failed to reassure a buyer's weakness or resolve a buyer's fear, which amounts to the same thing.

The more precisely you spot the buyer's weakness and apply your closing pressure there, the surer you are of closing and the quicker you will close.

A wise sales manager once said: "There is no hope for the satisfied man." There is no chance to sell him either. Unless you find a customer dissatisfied (which will be easy) or make him dissatisfied (which is easier still), you can't close sales.

Problems are the weakness of most prospects, problems that nag them, problems they need help to solve. Guess who's just volunteered to help? That's right. You. The accommodating salesperson. You solve buyer problems, you close your sale.

Joe Bowlin, an erudite business executive in Fort Worth, recalls a salesperson who *didn't* tackle the prospect's problem.

"He came to see me, a likeable young fellow," said Joe. "He wanted to sell me a machine I needed in my business. He told me about his company's new model. I looked at the prospectus and told him I didn't like it.

"He did not know my problems and he didn't try to find out. Instead, he just said he was sure the machine would perform. Did he try to pin me down and find out why I didn't agree? Did he try to dig out my problem? No. He merely said it was a swell machine and he was sure it would solve my problems (which he didn't know and didn't try to discover).

"He didn't make a sale," concluded Joe. "No salesman ever makes a sale until he learns the buyer's problems—that is to say, his weakness."

THREE GREAT COMPLEXES

A complex is a subject or condition we have deep emotional feelings about. This deep feeling in a prospect is a weakness. Your knowledge of this complex gives you a strength.

The ego complex is the instinct of self-preservation. It shows itself in the way we assert ourselves, in our vanity, in our pride, in our fears.

The sex complex includes love, jealousy, the parental instinct.

The herd complex causes us to want to be with others. It causes us to feel loneliness and isolation in the absence of others. The herd complex builds friendships, gives us a sense of sympathy and confidence in others—or distrust. It governs our relationships with other human beings. You must recognize and isolate these buyer fears to close sales.

For many years salespeople went along blindly, sometimes making sales, more often not, wondering why the buyer was so changeable. One moment he was rational and genial. The next moment he was narrow, unreasonable, impossible.

You can probably recall many such incidents. You are getting along fine. You are sure he or she is going to buy—all signs point to it. The buyer agrees with everything you say.

Then suddenly the buyer veers completely around and becomes insulting and insolent. You cannot recollect anything that might have caused it. The change mystifies you. Why the rapid change?

Modern scientists have discovered why. At the moment of buying, the buyer is not normal. He or she becomes abnormal.

When you're closing, buyers don't think as they usually think, don't act as they usually act, aren't the same person they were a few moments before. They're entirely different.

Dr. Donald Laird, formerly of Colgate University, says buyer reactions at closing are more like a crowd than an individual. Crowds do not reason. Crowds are emotional. Crowds are easily led, easily influenced, easily controlled by a person who understands the difference between crowd and individual psychology.

At the moment of closing, you are not dealing with a normal, well-poised, serene, self-confident, individual—but with the touchy, critical, emotional crowd mind.

This knowledge will help you close sales. It will enable you to understand perfectly why the buyer is so critical, so unreasonable, why he or she says such strange and unseemly things.

To understand your buyer's fears and needs—why he acts like a crowd at closing time—get on his side of the desk. Look at your proposal from his viewpoint.

Here are six different ways your customer thinks as a crowd, from Dr. Vincent S. Flowers of North Texas State University, and Dr. Charles C. Hughes, a management consultant. Find out early on which group-thinking you're appealing. It'll improve your closing average.

1. *Tribalistic* customers have no personal buying values and blindly accept beliefs and preferences of an authority figure. Beliefs originate from a chieftain—a parent, husband, wife, or boss.

They'll purchase as long as your product does not violate tribal tradition. If buying personally they pay cash—they don't often have checks or credit cards. To sell this customer, you must be reassuring—not free-wheeling, rational, or objective. Help the customer maintain membership in the peer group, reinforcing continued respect of the tribal chieftain. Testimonials from public figures are effective here.

2. *The Egocentric* buyer rejects tribal values and becomes overly assertive. This rugged individual *becomes* the tribal

chieftain and says: "To hell with the rest of the world. I think for myself."

Sometimes this egocentric customer believes salespeople are out for a rip-off and counters by attempting to rip you off *first*. Anything goes in the Egocentric's effort to dominate and win.

Play the game according to Egocentric's values. If he plays con man, be a better con. If he plays tough-guy, be tougher. The Egocentric is generally not concerned about product dependability, durability, cost savings, or guarantees. He or she is more concerned about product appearance, delivery, status, and the product's ability to act as symbol of rugged individualism and power.

Once the Egocentric decides to buy, he or she wants delivery right now—not in 60 days.

Long-term involvement is not the Egocentric's style. Make complete financial arrangements each time. Don't expect repeat business to come easy.

3. *Conformist* buyers have difficulty accepting people with other values. They try to get others to accept their values. They usually subordinate themselves to a philosophy, cause, or religion. They tend toward disciplined vocations with clearly defined rules.

Conformists want product dependability, durability, cost savings, and guarantees. They buy brand names from reliable stable companies. They aren't trend-setters. They reluctantly make changes.

The best strategy: be business-like and straightforward. Your sales presentation should be well structured and organized. Point out "everybody is buying." Dress conservatively. Avoid comments on religion, politics, or sex. Set up an exact time for the presentation and adhere to it. Be precise in every detail.

4. *Manipulative* buyers thrive on gamemanship, politics, competition, entrepreneurial efforts. They measure success in possessions, status, money.

They appreciate a fast-paced presentation. They don't need all the details. Simply present to them the highlights and wait for questions. Make sure you have all the benefits in reserve when you present.

The manipulative customer will often play stump-the-salesperson. If you get stumped, you lose the game.

They try to negotiate price. They demand a written contract with escape clauses. The strategy: let them believe they've won the game—while you make the sale.

5. To *Sociocentrics*, getting along is more important than getting ahead. Approval of respected people is valued more than individual achievement.

In dealing with a Sociocentric, relate your product or service to society. Play down status symbols, power, or materialistic gains.

Present good taste, respectability, social approval, benefits to people. Be soft, tender, and subjective.

Sociocentrics prefer you as friend rather than salesperson. Be flexible. Don't threaten their sense of belonging. If you make the sale, they may take *you* to dinner.

6. *Existentials* must participate in the sale, not be an observer. Present the problem, give them access to information, let them make their own decisions.

They want to know about the problem-solving aspects of your proposal. The fee or price has only secondary importance.

Be flexible and spontaneous. Stress simplicity and sense-making ethics. Avoid overemphasis on conventionality, status symbols, conformity, profitability, power, or short-range benefits. Slant your presentation to gaining acceptance of yourself, your company, your product, and its effect on the customer and environment. Let conversation be free flowing. Don't try to force structure.

WATCH FOR ATTITUDE SHIFTS

You're explaining your proposal to a buyer. You're making good progress. He or she listens courteously. Intelligent questions show interest. But as you come nearer to the close, the attitude changes. The buyer seems dazed and turns critical, is easily offended, is uncertain of decisions, takes offense at trifles.

Sometimes the shrug of a shoulder will turn the buyer off. A harmless remark can be taken as an insult and throw off the sale.

The prospect has developed defenses against being sold. These defenses vary. One buyer may affect a cantankerous attitude. Another may follow the time-honored practice of kissing you out the door. A third may clam up. A fourth might put you on the defensive with cross questions. A fifth may ignore you.

Sometimes the customer will develop an overemphasized sense of his or her own importance—after all, salespeople cater to the customer all day. He "thinks he is somebody." Yet before he became a buyer, he was probably a modest personality. His overimportance has changed him entirely. Recognize this and make your sale in spite of it.

All these are defenses. To sell, you must see through tricks and penetrate the guard.

WHY BUYER DEFENSES?

All defenses trace back to one word: fear. The buyer is thinking:

- Am I making a mistake in buying what you sell?
- Will I get my money's worth?
- Shall I wait for a while before buying?
- Am I acting without sufficient thought?
- How do I know the seller is honest?
- Would it be better to save my money, not buy anything, get along as I am?
- Will I lose that hard-earned money?
- Should I talk it over with somebody else?

Fears. Fears. Fears crowd the mind, making the buyer unsure, filled with complexes, and adding difficulty to your work. You must overcome fears before you close. Buyer fears have one antidote and only one: reassurance.

THE POWER OF REASSURANCE

Reassure your buyers they are acting wisely with fore-thought, and are getting good value for the money. What you're asking them to buy is exactly what they ought to buy—in value, satisfaction, profit, gratification.

Exactly what is reassurance? Merely restoration of confidence. At the moment of buying, prospects' confidence wavers. Their courage in their own opinions and judgment becomes shaken. They need confidence and courage restored. They must have reassurance.

Reassure your customer by what you *do* (your actions and attitude) and by what you *say*. Your attitude engenders confidence and builds reassurance—the simple, well-poised attitude of the professional. It's the quiet, self-confident bearing of a person who knows. You must *know* you know. *Professional Attitude* is the first and most important asset in reassuring the customer.

The spoken word is, of course, also valuable. Recently I considered buying an unfamiliar office product. I was uncertain and doubtful. The astute salesperson recognized that. He saw I was in that last-minute buying complex and needed reassurance.

"I know just how you feel about this," he said. "You're not sure this machine will do what we modestly claim it will do. Isn't that true?"

I admitted it.

"In that case, test the machine out, and see for yourself what it will do," he continued. "Let us put one in your office. Test it against your present equipment. Let actual results determine your decision. That's the way to handle the matter, don't you think?"

This masterful salesmanship at a crucial time completely reassured me. I became imbued with his confidence. I told him to forget to test. I'd just buy the machine. And I did.

That effective salesperson recognized that unless he swept away those fears and doubts he wouldn't make the sale at all. Far better than talk, he made a bold sweeping action offer to let me be the judge. It worked.

When you perceive doubt in your prospect's mind, offer a bold test. Usually the prospect won't accept it. Your offer to test will be reassurance enough.

Evidence (facts, figures, letters from authorities or satisfied users, reports, photographs) reassures prospects at closing time. They crave evidence—evidence you must give to build or reestablish conviction.

Often doubt takes the form of questions. Don't buff your chances by not knowing how to give advice. The prospect who asks advice is in doubt. If you fail to produce advice, the buyer will get it from someone else. You lose the sale.

I was trying on suits in a clothing store. We (the salesperson and I) narrowed the choice down to two. I didn't know which I wanted. Buyer's doubts began to fill my mind. I needed advice and reassurance.

"Which one do you think I ought to buy?" I asked the salesperson.

"Well, that's up to you," he replied. "You'll be wearing it."

This was the most inept selling at a critical point I ever saw. Instead of reassuring me, he dashed my confidence. I walked out. A little advice could have made the sale.

The lesson is clear: when the prospect asks for advice, give it. Help him or her decide. Make it easy to buy.

LEARN FROM MAIL-ORDER

Read good mail-order advertising to see how to overcome fear. Effective mail-order ads are salesmanship-in-print and reassurance-in-print. Customers are seeking to avoid loss of popularity, lack of prestige, lack of security, lack of love.

Frank Brumbaugh, selling-by-mail expert, reminds us that the American consumer:

- Has money to spend
- Will buy if you appeal to basic needs and desires
- Tolerates short delays
- Is basically honest

- Is acquisitive but not genuinely ambitious
- Is somewhat lazy
- Wants everything made easy
- Wants knowledge served in easy doses
- Dislikes having to think
- Dislikes high-pressure or too-clever selling
- Responds to friendly approaches
- Does not like to write letters
- Is often a poor manager of time and money
- Is always looking for bargains
- Dislikes taking risks, but will gamble small amounts
- Desires security without effort or risk
- Is frustrated by the pattern of modern life
- Longs for the "good old days" or thinks he does
- Is unsophisticated but unwilling to admit it
- Is afraid of anything he or she does not understand
- Is superstitious but unwilling to admit it
- Is often suspicious
- Often acts illogically
- Likes to be the first to own something new
- Has a sense of humor
- Is interested in sex and receptive to its appeal if handled smoothly
- Has a secret Walter Mitty complex
- Wants to add to his or her comfort
- Is interested in adding beauty to his or her surroundings
- Wants to save time

"Basic instincts and emotions of the customer do not change," Brumbaugh says. "These are reliable and as constant as the sun and the moon. Products or services directed to these instincts and emotions will get results as long as man inhabits the earth."

How valuable for the salesperson appealing to basic needs and seeking to overcome fears!

UNCOVER REAL NEEDS

Expert closers zero in on a customer's real needs—which may not be the same as his or her *expressed* needs.

George Higpen, an outdoor advertising salesperson in Nebraska, called on Samuel Geist, a department store owner. The prospect put up quite a struggle. Several times he told Higpen: "Listen, I don't want any personal publicity. So just forget about that."

Actually, Higpen hadn't planned a campaign based on personality. But after Geist repeated it several times—"no personal publicity"—Higpen got a glimmer of the *real* need. He came back with a campaign built on Geist speaking out for his store on vital local issues. He closed the sale.

"Most people hate to admit they're seeking personal recognition," Higpen said. "They think it makes them look ego-involved. So they articulate the opposite of what they actually want. This is particularly true if the prospect repeats the same phrase several times. That's a dead giveaway."

Discover your prospect's *real* needs. Learn to recognize these human motivations. Convert them to closed sales:

- *Security* (monetary gain, freedom from financial worry)
- *Self-preservation* (safety and health for self and family)
- *Convenience* (comfort, more desirable use of time)
- *Avoidance of worry* (ease of mind, confidence)
- *Recognition* (social status, respectability, wish to be admired)
- *Self-improvement* (spiritual development, hunger for knowledge, intellectual stimulation)

These combined wants are present in many buying situations:

- *Food, Clothing, and Shelter.* Every civilized person is a consumer of these.
- *Luxury as Necessities.* In modern society, certain products have become "necessities," even though survival does not strictly require them. Examples: automobile, refrigerator, washer and dryer, telephone, bathtub and shower, household furniture.
- *Profit.* Convince the retailer he can sell more of your brand X than brand Y, or that he can make money selling your X.

The alert real estate salesperson points out the high return on small down payment. The mutual fund salesperson outlines growth patterns of the stock market, projects similar patterns into future years to project a healthy profit. The stockbroker demonstrates tax advantages of buying municipal bonds. Desire for profit and lack-of-security fear are mirror-images.

- *Business Efficiency.* An office machine salesperson shows the buyer his or her product saves time, eliminates errors, improves efficiency, and thus increases profits. He or she is appealing to security, convenience, and profit.

- *Peace of Mind.* Products of services that bring inner peace range from seat belts to old-age pensions to life insurance. The American public spends millions of dollars on preventive medicine each year. If your product guarantees serenity, you're mining a rich vein.

- *Recognition.* How many people buy homes, diamond rings, furs, and backyard swimming pools to impress others?

BASIC FEARS

To start with, buyers are afraid they'll lose money or not get their money's worth; that they are going to be cheated; that what you are trying to get them to buy costs more than they can afford.

Secondly, buyers are afraid the product or service might not be what it's represented to be and not worth the price. They're particularly doubtful when buying something new—a saddlebred horse, a blue zircon brooch, the first painting in an art collection.

Thirdly, buyers have large fears about what others might think. Perhaps his wife will ridicule him. Or the neighborhood will poke fun at her. Or someone the buyer respects will scoff at an unwise choice.

Most common of all concerns is the money fear. Money is the one subject most of us think about most of the time. We dread loss of money more than anything. The antidote for money fears: simple reassurance.

Money is measured more closely than anything else. To overcome fears about money, reassurance must consist of facts and figures. Show in black and white the buyer's getting good and true value. Testimonials—someone else's opinion—help overcome money fears. Of all selling techniques, none approaches the testimonial for effectiveness in establishing confidence and inspiring action. Testimonials reassure wavering prospects.

Your prospect's fears about the product itself usually trace back to poor salesmanship prior to closing. The first closing secret: build absolute and distinct understanding with the buyer before you attempt to close. If your buyer really understands the benefits of your proposal, there won't be any room for fear. The antidote for product fear is to do a good job of communicating understanding before you close.

If, in spite of your earnest attempt, the buyer is still doubtful, reintroduce evidence that proves the value of your product all over again.

Another cause of fear is what others will think. You must sweep away these fears. Reassure the buyer he or she is doing the right thing in the eyes of someone whom the buyer respects or fears. Show how this action will bring credit to the buyer. Show that others will think it's a wise decision. Buyers are human enough to want approval. Prove they'll get it. Show the buyer a list of respected companies or executives who have bought.

SELLING WITH RIDICULE

One office equipment salesperson used ridicule—usually a hazardous option—in selling files to an airline's regional office.

"The office manager wanted to buy new files," the salesperson said. "But he was afraid his superiors would criticize him. So the sale bogged down. I called repeatedly. I argued myself blue in the face about the folly of keeping obsolete, cheap filing cabinets in a modern office. No good."

The salesperson continued, "I figured if I could appeal to his pride, I could banish fears. So I took a bold step. On my next visit, I slapped his tinny filing cabinets and said (loud for everybody in the office to hear): 'T.C., T.C.'

"What do you mean 'T.C.?'" the office manager said.

"Why, Tin Can, Tin Can. That's the filing cabinets in this office—T.Cs.," the salesperson said.

That impressed the prospect. He sat there thinking hard. Two days later he called and asked the salesperson to replace those cheap cabinets with the best in the line.

"The buyer's fears of spending money were more than offset by the blow to his pride at running an office with tin cans for files," the salesperson said. "Of course, I wouldn't do this to all my prospects. It is dangerous. But I knew my man and anticipated his reaction."

SELLING THE EMPIRE

Joseph P. Day, the great New York auctioneer, sold the Empire Building to Judge Elbert Gary, founder of U.S. Steel, by overcoming fear.

Judge Gary wanted to buy a building, but nothing Day showed pleased Judge Gary. Day sensed that, deep down in his heart, Judge Gary wanted to buy the building where U.S. Steel had always rented offices. He also sensed the obstacle was Gary's fear of what other officers would think—officers who wanted "something modern." But Gary never said this in words.

Instead he found objections to the Empire building—old-fashioned woodwork, poor location, etc. Day knew these arguments did not originate with Judge Gary. Day also knew he would have to help his prospect overcome those objections. So he said quietly: "Judge, where was your office when you first came to New York?"

Judge Gary paused: "In this very building."

Then the salesperson asked: "Where was U.S. Steel formed?"

"Right here, in this very office," he replied.

Both remained silent. At last, Judge Gary spoke. "Nearly all of my junior officers want to leave this building. But it's our home. We were born here. We've grown up here. And here is where we are going to stay."

Day had helped Judge Gary articulate his defense. Inside half an hour the deal was closed. The shrewd Day let the Judge sell himself. He helped the prospect overcome fears of others' opinions so he could decide to buy.

Buyers on the verge of spending money must be reassured they're acting wisely and in their own best interest. Buyers express fears differently. They may become sullen, suspicious, cantankerous. They may be quiet—even poker-faced.

Just the same, buyers need your reassurance, your confirmation that the transaction is the wisest thing they could do under the circumstances. Every buyer has fears, and until you overcome them, you will find difficulty in closing your sale.

ORDER-BLANK FEAR

A customer who has been listening and nodding will suddenly run like a bandit when you flash the order blank. Many orders are completely spoiled when the salesperson introduces the order blank in the wrong way or at the wrong time. The sight of it can drive buying clear out of the customer's mind.

The order form triggers abnormal emotions in buyers. They don't reason that signing an order is a safe, logical thing to do. They don't reason at all. They just respond to fear—of putting names down in black and white. They're scared witless.

Handling the order blank so it will not frighten the buyer is simple. Introduce it early in the sale. Let the buyer get gradually accustomed to it. Bring it out, handle it casually, quote from it, point to it, read from it, keep it in plain sight during the whole interview. Then, when the time comes to sign, the buyer won't run. It is common and familiar. There's no reason to fear it.

One savvy sales manager worked out a book that combines order blank and price sheet with prices on the cover. In his field, prices change daily. The first thing the customer wants to know is the price of this or that. The salesperson puts the book on the counter, opens it, and quotes the price.

The customer is face to face with the order blank without knowing it. The next logical step is to write in the order. It's all so simple, so natural, so logical. It avoids the artificial barrier at closing time.

CROWD PSYCHOLOGY

Remember the buyer's mind at closing is more a crowd than an individual. Crowds are fearful. Crowds are capable of heroism. Crowds are equally capable of great cowardice. Ten minutes after heroically hitting an invasion beach, an infantry company will suddenly become stricken with terror, cast down its weapons, and run. Often there's no logical reason for it. It's just that the crowd is unpredictable.

One of the world's great authority upon crowds, Gustave Le Bon, says to handle crowds—and this applies to handling individuals at the point of buying, for theirs is the crowd mind—you must:

- Assure by affirmation
- Make the crowd understand by repetition
- Provide inspiration by setting the example

Every time you close a sale, quote reassurance phrases and testimonials to allay and overcome buyer fears. Repeat the same ideas in different words to drive fears from the buyer's consciousness. Inspire by example with self-confidence, by your enthusiasm for your product, by your obvious knowledge of what it will do for your prospect.

You now possess the groundwork for closing more sales—by turning buyer weakness into closing strength.

CLOSING IN THE RIGHT PSYCHOLOGICAL CLIMATE

7

SALESPEOPLE once thought they could read character by the length of a prospect's nose or the shape of the cranium. Today we judge prospects by watching them in action and by listening to their reactions—not by studying them as specimens in the zoo.

For appearance alone often deceives.

A seedy character once walked into a Miami real estate office. He looked like a farmer spending the winter in Florida.

In fact, he *was* a farmer from Iowa, retired and "looking for a place to put a little money."

Fortunately, at the counter was a customer relations lady who refused to prejudge. She looked beyond the misshapen hat and clumsy shoes.

She "cultivated" the farmer courteously, taking pains to explain the different property listings.

She noted he was a quiet, slow talker. That gave her a clue in handling him—don't rush him.

She noticed he was conservative in his thinking—don't pull any get-rich-quick stunts.

Her diligence paid off. The retired man bought a lot. But that wasn't the end. He kept on buying.

They made progress: she kept watching, watching, watching for clues.

In the end she won his full confidence and sold him $2 million worth of real estate.

Each prospect gives clues.

Watch these clues and close sales.

VERSATILITY IS THE KEY

Think you're not cut out to sell certain types of buyers? Don't believe it. A good salesperson is versatile. Adjust yourself to the buyer's mood or mentality. Take buyers as they come—the hard-boiled, the easy, the suspicious, the pleasant, the fast, the slow. They're all workable to a person who really knows how to close.

There are different types of buyers, however, and good closers plan ways to handle each. Establish the right psychological climate to close each buyer.

Rate of thinking varies with buyers. One buyer gives you the feeling he's thinking ahead of you. The next has to be dragged along behind you. Another seems to keep up with you and sees things pretty much as you explain them.

If you talk too fast to the slow-thinker, your selling can't reach optimum efficiency. Talking too slowly to the person who thinks fast is almost as bad because you irritate the buyer. Early in every sale gauge your presentation to your buyer's rate of thinking.

The buyer who makes up his mind in reasonable time, or decides things quickly, causes little trouble. You like to call on those buyers. You don't like the indecisive buyer or the buyer who can't make up his mind at all.

Yet the raw material you make sales out of—day in and day out—consists of buyers of this kind. Adjust your sales presentation to the tempo of the listener. If you don't, you don't sell.

Classify buyers by how they react to your presentation. (Probably they react to life the same way, but you're concerned with them only in the sales setting.)

CLOSING FOUR BASIC TYPES

Dr. Paul Mok of Dallas divides customers into four basic types: *intuitors, thinkers, feelers,* and *sensors.* Further, he says, you as a salesperson are also predominately one of those four types.

"First find out what type you are—*then* what type your customer is," Dr. Mok says. "Then alter your behavior to harmonize with the buyer's. It works."

First look at the four types:

- The *Intuitor* speculates, imagines, envisions. For you to succeed, he or she must perceive your product as an instrument for accomplishing his or her long-range goal and master plan.

- The *Thinker* rationalizes, deduces, analyzes, weighs options. He or she must perceive your product as proved, tested, and reliable—reflective of his or her own analytical judgment.

- The *Feeler* emphathizes, remembers, reacts, relates. He or she must perceive you as a personal ally. He or she buys based on judgments of people.

- The *Sensor* makes decisions on what his or her senses tell about your product *right now.* He's striving, driving, and competing to get that edge. He must perceive your product as providing him with a tool to win his game.

Remember, there are few pure styles. Most people use varying blends at different times. But you are most naturally one dominant style.

No one style is good or bad. Each style can be used effectively or ineffectively. There are positive characteristics associated with each and also negative characteristics, usually resulting from overextending the positive. (Any strength carried to extreme can become a weakness.)

"Think of your radio's volume-control knob," Dr. Mok says. "The more you turn it, the louder the sound. Turn it far enough and the sound gets distorted. Strengths work the same way."

An overextended *Sensor* becomes so competitive and bottom-line oriented that customers see him as cutthroat, power-hungry, money-hungry.

The overly cautious *Thinker* becomes so detailed and analytical he never makes a decision. He insists first on holding the proposition up to the light from every possible angle. He may thus be seen as rigid, nitpicky, inflexible.

Intuitor's originality may be viewed as unrealistic. His broad-gauged, big-picture imaginative way of visualizing may seem scattered or impractical.

Feeler's spontaneous, emphatic, probing, and introspective behavior may seem overly impulsive, too personalized, sentimental, or subjective.

How to tell your prospect's style? Look at the condition of his or her desk, pictures on the wall, general office decor, attire. Listen to the way he or she talks on the phone. Read his or her letters and memos. Look for clues in speech:

Intuitors: wordy but aloof, impersonal

Thinkers: ordered, measured, business-like manner

Feelers: warm and friendly

Sensors: abrupt, to the point, controls the conversation

Clues in writing:

Intuitors: writes as he or she speaks in intellectual, often abstract, terms

Thinkers: well-organized, structured, specific, tight

Feelers: short and highly personalized

Sensors: curt, action-oriented, urgent

Clues in office decor:

Intuitors: futuristic, think-tank style

Thinkers: correct, nondistracting, tasteful but conventional

Feelers: informal, homey, warm, personalized

Sensors: cluttered

"Once you know your style and your prospect's style, do everything to make them cooperate, not conflict," Dr. Mok says. "Flex your style. Harmonize with your prospect. Suddenly you're both on the same wavelength. Nobody's computer is flashing *reject*."

CLOSING WITH STYLE-FLEX

Here, from Dr. Mok's archives, are ways nine successful salespeople have closed sales by analyzing the customer's style and adapting their own style to match.

1. A Thinker (soft-drink account executive) discovered his prospect was a Feeler and digested his one and a half hour presentation into four minutes. He landed an order for 150,000 gallons of syrup.

2. A Midwest heavy equipment salesman resented his rude, crude, interrupting prospect. Then he realized his prospect was a bottom-line Sensor. He stopped bombarding facts the man didn't want and got a $100,000 order in 18 minutes.

3. A strong Thinker CPA, realizing his prospective client was a Feeler, modified his normal approach of presenting a detailed outline of his services. Instead he invited the prospect to his own office to "meet the staff and get a feeling for the people who would be working on your account." The prospect signed an engagement letter the same day.

4. An Intuitor salesperson for a major financial magazine shifted from his usual conceptual approach to get on a Thinker's wavelength. He presented a 90-minute detailed presentation including advertising options and variations. He left a detailed proposal and asked the prospect to analyze and review it. Two days later the prospect signed a contract for $160,000.

5. A land development salesperson, gauging his prospect as a heavy Intuitor, shifted his normal bottom-line chance-of-a-lifetime, the-price-is-going-up approach. He spent 15 minutes talking about esthetic value of the land. He encouraged the prospect to envision the property ten years hence. The salesperson wrote the contract and got a down payment 20 minutes later.

6. A life insurance agent found her prospect bored and restless as she systematically went through her 35-page presen-

tation. Sensing the prospect as a strong Sensor, the salesperson abruptly closed her portfolio and said:

"Let's look at the bottom line, what it's going to cost you, and what your spouse gets should something happen to you."

Ten minutes later she wrote a $200,000 straight life policy.

7. A computer hardware salesperson made a presentation to three owners of a medium-sized commercial art studio. In his usual Thinker style, the salesperson arrived in his three-piece suit with three different, detailed proposals in his attaché case.

To his surprise, the three owners were late and all wore jeans and running shoes. Quickly sensing these three owners as Intuitors not likely to sit still long, the salesperson made a brief opening philosophy of his company, took off his coat and unbuttoned his vest, indicated he preferred to have his customers design their own system. He asked the owners to go to the blackboard (located in their office) and, using their own imagination, diagram a system that would handle their needs.

"Don't worry about hardware names. Just indicate what you want it to do," the salesperson said. When the owners finished, the salesperson went to their design, and using a red marker, put the name of his hardware component over the appropriate place in the design.

He then stepped back, looked at the design and said: "Gentlemen, that's a helluva system."

Following a quick demonstration of his components, the owners placed an order. They never saw his detailed proposal.

8. An account representative for a major investment firm started to stylize his correspondence and found that by sending Feeler notes to Feelers, one paragraph of "suggested action" notes to Sensors, and longer speculative letters to Intuitors (he saved the firm's detailed market analysis newsletter for the Thinkers), his level of closes increased dramatically.

9. An industrial products salesperson who did much telephone selling trained his secretary to identify a caller's probable style based on his or her greeting, tone of voice, and basic phone manner. This enabled him to begin style-flexing right away.

The salesperson not only saved valuable time but also found that he was getting more repeat business than in the past.

Dr. Mok, himself a master salesperson as well as pioneering sales trainer, says you can become an expert in analyzing personality types—and close more sales each month because of it.

"That's why I call it style-flex," Dr. Mok says. "Learn your predominant style. That's what you are most natural in. Discern the customer's style, then match your style to his during this encounter. It closes sales."

It makes sense. After all, each person prefers to buy from the same kind of personality type. Don't *you*?

PUT PERSONALITY QUIRKS TO WORK

In addition to the broad personality styles just discussed, you'll frequently run into smaller quirks of human nature that at first appear to be barriers to closing. Once you understand them, however, you can convert these quirks to your advantage.

• Take the *Close Dealer*, for example. He's never expansive or magnanimous, but always backward and niggardly and seeking an advantage. You probably can recollect a number of these buyers, always on the defensive, always making you uncomfortable with their picayunish attitudes and reactions. Don't try to push the *Close Dealer* too much. You can't high-pressure him—but you can lead him.

• At the opposite pole there's the *Egotist*. He's sure he knows more about what you're selling than you do. He angers you by telling you about your goods or your job. He often thinks he's the quintessence of buying skill. Actually, the *Egotist* carries with him the seeds of his undoing. Play on his egotism. Ask him advice. Consult him on details. Compliment him. Praise him. Do these things and you'll close.

• Then there's *Facts Only*. Emotional appeals leave this buyer cold. He deludes himself that he lives in a world of reason. To sell him, ply him with facts, crowd him with facts, appeal to his reason. Then he isn't so tough.

• *Selling the money-minded*. Bob Schiffman racked up a top record as a Cadillac salesman in New York—one of the world's toughest and richest car markets. He sold 100 cars a year and earned a place in General Motors' famous Crest Club, an elite membership limited to 200 salesfolk at any given time.

Schiffman closed sales by always assuming his prospect was money-minded.

"No matter what your product or service, work in a financial benefit and sell that," Schiffman advises. "This is particularly true if you sell business executives. To them, the world *is* a money package."

Schiffman always did his financial homework before facing his customer. One day, the president of a manufacturing company wasn't responding to Schiffman's approach on a new Cadillac.

Schiffman took figures out of his pocket.

"Mr. Leiter," he said. "I've just done some arithmetic for you. If you take this $8000 car by trading in last year's car for $6,000, you can make up the extra $2000 in tax savings. Here's how the figures work."

The man signed up.

"I even had customers I could show how to *make* money by trading cars," Schiffman says. "How's that for a benefit?"

Bob Schiffman never sold cars. He sold financial benefits. Come to think of it, he was merely flexing his style to suit the customers—just like Dr. Paul Mok advises.

• *Mr. Indecision* is probably the buyer you like the least. He shakes his head, expresses doubts and fears, and says: "I just don't know." He won't make up his mind. What then? Make up your mind *first*, his mind *second*, and push him to a close. Apply a little more pressure than you would to any other type.

• The *Chiseler* is always seeking some advantage. He won't buy unless he is getting a better deal than anyone else. He's always looking for bargains, price, price, price, price. You soon learn to handle him. Your product is always "made-to-order" for this buyer. He almost always responds favorably to it. For him, it is what doctors call a specific.

• Then there's *Mr. Irascible.* He's rude, rough, human. He rants, he swears, he bluffs, he curses. If you are timid, you won't sell him. Stay with him until the storm blows over. Once you crack *Mr. Irascible,* he's usually soft at the core, not hard to sell at all.

• You don't like the *Complainer,* either. No matter what you do, nothing is right. He always has a pet grievance. He suffers from self-persecution, thinks your organization works 24 hours a day to take advantage of him. You can't make light of his grievance.

Listen to him with patience and sympathy. Let him talk himself out of his grievance, and then he won't be very difficult. But watch him—he'll try to get you to take *his* side against your firm's. This a good salesperson never does.

• Probably you don't like *Moody* either—you know, the buyer who's all smiles and backslaps one time and then barely speaks to you the next. You can't tell which way he's going to jump. Use patience and understanding and be willing to follow his lead. Taking your clue from him will go a long way toward selling *Moody.*

• *Closing the Bargain-Minded.* In an unforgettable scene in *Oliver Twist,* Oliver astonishes the workhouse managers by asking for *more* at breakfast.

More! Isn't that what many buyers want above all? And isn't it your job to provide *more* and close sales in the process? *More* is all in the way you present it.

Walter A. Lowen, a pioneering headhunter, once saw an astonishing sight in a candy store. One salesgirl was waiting on a line of shoppers. Other salesgirls were idle. Customers appeared quite happy waiting in the busy line.

When the crowd thinned, Lowen asked the successful girl: "Why do they come to you in preference to the others?"

The popular girl lifted her scoop. "It's easy," she said. "The other girls scoop up more than a pound of candy and then take some away to make exact weight. I scoop up *less* than a pound and *add* to it."

Each girl allocated customers one pound. But the ace salesgirl gave *more*. Think about it. There are ways to give your customers more, no matter what you sell. You can close sales with *more* when you create the right psychological climate.

LET PROSPECTS TELL YOU THE RIGHT TIME TO CLOSE

8

A FEW YEARS BACK, in salesmanship theory, you waited for the psychological moment to close the sale. It was the exact moment when everything was right. The prospect's mind was attuned. His resistances were flattened. His purse was open. He was yours.

Today, of course, this is too simplistic. The psychological moment has been displaced by another belief: the right moment to close is now! You close when the prospect tells you to close.

There is not one time when a close is in order. There may be 100. Good salespeople close twice as fast and thus close twice as much.

By using the trial close (merely an innocuous closing technique) you determine if the buyer is ready. If so, you've got yourself an order. If not, go on into the sale, build it, and try again. Always be ready to close.

"A decent boldness," wrote Lord Chesterfield in one of his famous letters, "always wins respect."

Boldness in selling wins respect and orders. There are times in every sale when you have nothing to lose by taking a chance and everything to win. Here's how decent boldness works.

The salesman, an old pro, ran into unexpected resistance. The buyer trotted out all the objections, including a few neat little insults.

The sale seemed shot.

The old pro stopped his prospect. "Wait just a minute, will you, while I write this up."

"Write what up?" asked the prospect.

"Your order."

"But I am not going to buy, I just told you that."

"I know, I know. I heard you. But what you said convinces me you need my line."

Boldness won. The prospect signed!

When you think the buyer is ready for the close, push forward with confidence. Act on the positive assumption you are going to sell. Say nothing and do nothing unless it's predicated upon the belief that your customer is going to buy. Assume the only real question is *when*.

That's the closing procedure. You'll have a great deal more confidence in yourself when you learn how to tell when the buyer's ready. All you do is keep your eyes open for buying signals.

There may be a few hard-boiled poker faces whose appearance is a perfect defense against salesmanship. But most buyers will reveal by little things they're ready for the close. When these signals occur it's your cue to march in and try for the close.

SPOKEN AND UNSPOKEN CLUES

Closing signals are both spoken and unspoken: either words or actions, including facial expressions, or both. Not all buyers are accommodating enough to tell you in so many words. Nevertheless, they reveal exactly what's going on in their minds. How do you read the signs?

• *Expressions.* Good closers study facial expressions as carefully as FBI agents quiz a suspect. Certain expressions—particularly in the eyes—reveal conviction and desire. No one can describe them exactly for you. You learn from experience what they are. Be on the alert to these expressions and be quick to act on them.

• *Body language* may be obvious or it may be guarded. But most buyers definitely express their minds by what they do.

The buyer steps back for a better look at the merchandise, or he takes it over to the light where he can examine it more closely.

The prospect scratches his chin in indecision. Or he examines the sample. Or he looks at the label.

He lifts the product, pushes the keys, or pulls the lever. He picks up the literature once more and becomes absorbed by it.

He picks up the contract blank and reads a clause or two carefully.

Mind you, he or she may not say a word. Words aren't necessary. Actions show he has reached the point where a close is in order. He wants you to step in and make up his mind.

Few prospects will tell you right out they're ready to buy. They're much too cagey.

SELLING AN UNPROVED SERVICE

A most unusual closer worked for Hubert Bermont, who sells a management consulting service.

Bermont, based in Washington, D.C., had just formed his own consulting company. He had the office, the letterhead, the telephone—but not the clients. Clearly, to stay alive he had to sell.

"I made three telephone calls to former colleagues," Bermont relates. "In each case, when asked why I wanted an appointment, I said I was seeking consulting work."

So what happened? Came the next fatal question: "Whom are you doing consulting work for now?" Bermont had to say: "No one."

Bermont decided to steal a page from Mark Twain. After unsuccessfully trying to mine silver in the desert, Twain arrived penniless in San Francisco. He went to the most illustrious newspaper and applied for a job as reporter.

No jobs, he was told, because there was no money. Twain told the editor he required no compensation—he only wanted to write for free.

Twain immediately got a job under those terms. His stories won wide readership. He then resigned, reminding his angry employers he was receiving no compensation. The newspaper put him on salary and made him a foreign correspondent.

Bermont decided to do something similar. He went to the most prestigious company in his field. Bermont laid out an entire workload and told the officer he wanted to do this free of charge. He told him honestly why. The client gladly accepted.

"I worked like hell for that firm, setting up meetings, solving problems, making projections, and filing daily progress reports," Bermont says.

Within two weeks, the boss visited Bermont. Not only were they impressed with his work, they were overwhelmed by his approach. He asked what kind of retainer Bermont wanted. Bermont named a price. They shook on it.

Bermont waited for buying signals. Granted, this is an unusual case. Not every salesperson can offer his product free. But you can offer free service, free help, free assistance. Sometimes it pays. Offer something free and wait for buying signals.

P.S. In his next sales call, when asked about clients, Bermont gave the biggest name in the field.

CLOSING THE CAPTIVE PROSPECT

When you get a buyer all alone—with no interference—you have a closer's dream. However, play it just right. Don't appear to take unfair advantage. Even with a captive audience, wait until the customer tells you when to close.

Glenn O. Benz, sales director for Northland Aluminum Products, invited Jimmy Peterson, Pillsbury's grocery products division vice-president, on a weekend cruise.

Benz' mission: get Pillsbury to name a cake mix after the Bundt aluminum pan Northland had just produced.

"The weather was perfect—clear, cool," Benz recalls. "Leaves at their height of fall brilliance. No TV, no telephone, no commercial radio, no noise."

They boarded the yacht. Peterson, a former naval officer, was at the helm. Can you imagine a more captive audience? Further, Peterson asked Benz:

"How can you help our business grow?"

As the yacht maneuvered between the islands, Benz presented the plan: name the cake mix after the Bundt pan. Then he dropped the subject.

After two days of sailing, they headed for home.

Late Sunday night back in the car, they ran into an early fall blizzard. Visibility was limited. The only sounds were the purr of the engine and the swishing of windshield wipers. Benz was listening.

About 2 a.m., Peterson broke the silence, saying: "It's a great idea. Come over to the office about 8 a.m. I'll get our staff involved and work out details with the marketing manager."

The rest is history.

Bundt Cake Mix captured a large share of the market for several years. Pillsbury's one-minute TV commercial was shown coast-to-coast. Every cook needed a pan to make this revolutionary cake.

Sales of Bundt pans soared beyond imagination. Benz was back-ordered for several months. He sold to department stores, discounters, drug stores, grocery stores, mail-order catalog showrooms, distributors, wholesalers, and the military.

Waiting for the customer to tell Benz when to close was an important factor. Another: selling the total marketing concept, not just a cake pan.

"Details were precisely executed," recalls Benz, who later became director of marketing and sales for Shamrock Industries' Housewares division. "The comprehensive sale required countless personal calls, personal participation in store demonstrations, personal presentations to military/catalog/showroom buying committees, and personal calls to premium warehouses and distributors.

"It proves, once again, that personal closing will always be with us. There's no substitute for personal selling."

COLUMBO—NOT JAMES BOND

Probably the greatest enthusiast about listening for closing signals is David H. Sandler. Sandler, a sales trainer in Stevenson, MD, is also a first-rate salesman himself.

Sandler believes that 95 percent of salespeople close sales all wrong. Sandler does not believe in hard sell.

"People buy in spite of hard sell, not because of it," he says.

Normally in a selling interview, the salesman urges the customer to buy and the customer urges the salesman to leave him alone.

"It's too expensive" or "I'll have to think it over" or "I'd better discuss this with my partner" are standard objections. Many sales managers issue 27 different answers for handling them.

Not Sandler. See how it works as Sandler refutes standard accepted assumptions.

• *Assumption one:* Salespeople should be extroverted.
Sandler: All wrong. The more experienced the salesperson, the more he or she knows to keep a low profile.

• *Assumption two:* The salesperson must learn everything about his or her product.
Sandler: This usually translates into the salesperson trying to impress his or her prospect with how much he or she knows. Most salespeople want to describe product benefits before the prospect is even interested.

• *Assumption three:* Always ask for the order and be prepared for objections.
Sandler: Never ask for the order and always bring up objections before the customer thinks of them.

• *Assumption four:* The super salesperson must be a great talker.

Sandler: The super salesperson is a great listener.

The effective salesman must practice the exact opposite of these common assumptions.

Most people erroneously think of the super salesperson as a James Bond character—attractive, smooth, debonair. Sandler recommends the sales approach of Columbo, the television detective. Columbo appears rumpled, absent-minded, awkward. Suspects think he's bumbling and stupid until they reveal their guilt.

"Columbo makes no assumptions," Sandler says. "He doesn't try to read other people's minds. He gets what he wants by asking questions, more questions, and then a few more questions. That's what selling is all about. Asking, not telling. Listening, not talking.

"Selling isn't a dog and a pony show. The best sales are the ones you never see, where the customer does the work and the salesperson simply asks questions and writes up the order at the customer's instructions.

"Remember the law of inertia: a body in motion tends to stay in motion. If your prospect is swinging against you, don't try to block him or you'll both collide. Gently lead him to a neutral position. Then start the swing in your favor. Do this by disarming him. Say precisely what he doesn't expect."

If a prospect says he's not interested, he expects the salesperson to tell him why he should be. The tug-of-war begins. Prospects says no, salesperson says yes—back and forth—until one side gives up.

Here's how Sandler handles an unfriendly prospect.

Prospect: "I'm not interested."

Salesperson: "Maybe you shouldn't be. But let me ask you a question, what is it that you're really interested in?"

Prospect: "I really don't want to spend the money...."

Salesperson: "Well maybe you shouldn't. Let me ask you this—how much were you hoping to spend?"

"At this point," Sandler said, "we've gone from no to neutral and it's just a matter of time before the customer swings to yes. We accomplish this by saying maybe he shouldn't be interested, which surprises him, and then by asking him questions."

A prospect expects a gung-ho salesperson. If the salesperson, instead, refuses to sell, and tries to discourage buying, the prospect will almost always ask the salesperson to start selling. Instead of resisting the sale, the prospect is pulling for it.

"When the so-called super salesman meets a prospect, it usually looks like a gladiatorial battle," Sandler says. "The customer winds up on the floor scarred and bruised. The salesperson, huffing and puffing because of his gymnastics, is lying on top of him thinking he's done a good job."

"In good selling, you should behave just the opposite," says Sandler. "Let the customer do all the work. He talks. You listen."

Sandler's approach may not work for everyone. But isn't he just saying—one more time—you should listen for clues to close?

LEARN FROM ASTUTE RETAILERS

It's the fashion among business-to-business salesfolk to scoff at retailers as "order takers" who are "not in *real* selling." Don K. Covington, president of Harbor Sales Company, Baltimore, thinks this is a mistake. He advises his salesforce to look at the best retailers for inspiration.

Covington, also regional vice-president of Sales and Marketing Executives International, cites this retail evidence of watching for customer buying signals.

> My wife frequently asks me to pick up items from the bakery "on the way home." Actually, it's miles out of the way and parking is difficult.
>
> So, under pressure of time and fuel economy, I stop at a more convenient store with parking, self-service, speedy electronic check-out, and quality goods.
>
> Mission accomplished. Well, almost.
>
> When questioned, I admit the product did not come from ABC but from the more convenient XYZ store. At that point, the product immediately becomes inferior, by my wife's standard. How come? I found out why when I accompanied her grocery shopping.

I watched her careful searching for special sale items, rebate offers, matching of discount coupons, unit pricing comparisons.

"Why skip the baked goods section?" I asked.

"We are going to the ABC bakery to get a pie," she said.

Good, I thought, now we'll see the reason for ABC's sales success.

When we got there, happy customers were standing three deep at the counter. Each had a take-a-number rotation slip. Our number—84—and they were serving 56.

When our number was finally called, my wife announced: "We'll wait for Mary." Ah ha, so Mary's the secret ingredient, I thought.

Mary said a gracious goodbye to her departing customer. She turned to us and opened: "Hello, Mrs. Covington (personal recognition). How may I help you today?"

"I'm interested in pie," my wife said. "Hope you have cherry. Our son and his family are coming to dinner. That's his favorite."

"Well," Mary said, "I'm certainly glad you came to ABC (brand identification) today, Mrs. Covington. This very morning our baker made some of his finest cherry pies."

She went to a rack of a dozen cherry pies, picked up one, but hesitated. She returned and took another pie. She looked directly into her customer's eyes and proudly said:

"This is the *very* pie for you, Mrs. Covington!"

Now all the cherry pies on that rack were undoubtedly made at the same time. However a satisfied ABC customer reveled in the knowledge that her pie was especially selected and was thereby outstanding.

Good closing is a joy to behold.

Only 4 percent of buyers buy according to price. Yet we frequently spend all our productive time selling price to the other 96 percent. Let's start focusing on the fundamental role of personal salesmanship. It's more important than ever.

Now you don't sell pies, of course. But do you listen that closely—and relate that well—to your customers? If you do, you're closing a lot of sales already. (If not, a word to the wise.)

STOP TALKING: WRITE ORDER

Never, never talk after you have decided the buyer is ready for the close. If you do, you'll lose sales.

The important thing to remember is to close just as soon as you can. Don't permit any sale to drag one second longer than necessary—even if you have delivered only half your sales talk and made only a few of your sales points, or even if you feel you have not advanced your strongest arguments. If you get any hint that indicates the close is at hand, drop everything, stop talking, step in—and try to close.

Although it's difficult to know just when the time for a close has arrived, with a little practice you can get the feel of the situation.

Experienced salespeople, trained in watching the prospect for the buying signs, can tell whether the prospect is favorable, unfavorable, or indifferent. They naturally like to see as many *favorable* prospects as they can. They don't particularly worry when a prospect is *unfavorable:* they know they have to keep working on him.

But we all dread the *indifferent* prospect. He doesn't respond no matter what you tell him. He's the prospect who needs the most work. Regardless of the situation, the minute you feel it's time for the close, try it. You'll be surprised how often it works.

FOREVER ON THE ALERT

Signals in words are obviously the clearest, plainest clues. But the close is not so hard to find out. Remember the other forms the closing signals may take. Keep a sharp watch for them when they occur.

When you begin looking for these signals and recognizing them, you will find it comparatively easy to decide when to close. The more experienced you become in watching for these signals, the easier you'll recognize them. They will become second nature.

Start watching for signals. Practice the art of recognizing them. In the fine art of closing sales remember this guiding rule. "Nothing is more important than being forever on the alert." That advice was first offered a century ago by Henry David Thoreau. No one before or since ever better counseled the salesperson on the closing sales—be forever on the alert.

HERE'S YOUR MASTER CLOSING FORMULA

9

By now I hope you have reached this conclusion: that closing sales and being a good closer are not hit-or-miss. Good closers aren't winds-of-chance salespeople. They follow a formula. They know the value of everything they do. They are precisionists. You must be too.

Their precision shows up most in the way they adhere to and follow a definite closing formula. Learn it now and use it the rest of your selling life.

The Master Closing Formula is venerated by every good closer that ever lived. It has just four simple parts. Yet by adhering to these, by following them as rules, great closers achieve selling miracles and make fortunes. So can you.

The classic four-part formula is:

1. Make every call a selling call.
2. Try early in every sale for a close.
3. Close on every resistance.
4. Keep trying time after time.

Nothing new or complicated about that formula. But there is something miraculous about it—if you use it time and time again.

Let's dissect the formula step by step.

1. EVERY CALL A SELLING CALL

What use is it to make a call if you don't try to make a sale? You aren't a visitor or an office loafer. (Yet some salespeople qualify for both these titles.) You are a closer. Your one purpose in life is to bring in an order.

So adopt this as your first rule—make every call a selling call. That one rule will get you over, forever, the notion that you are a *goodwill ambassador*, a *missionary*. It will label you with the only name that will ever do you any good: a *salesperson* who specializes in *closing*, salesmanship's moment of truth.

Every so often—even the best closers miss one now and then—you'll end up in a goodwill or missionary role. Let it be accidental and abhorrent when you do.

If you make every call a selling call, you obviously will try to close on every call, won't you? That will lead you to the second rule.

2. TRY TO CLOSE EARLY IN EVERY SALE

You know Hugh Bell's feeling about closing early. It's the policy of all good closers. Their feelings are try early, sometimes with your first words!

Tom Cook was the strongest and most urgent closer of them all. He started every sale with an appeal for an order—his very first words. Buyers cannot deny a salesperson like that very long.

Tom Cook's method was as device-free as a child asking for a quarter to buy candy.

"Mr. Phillips, I am calling on you today to get your order for my service, provided I can prove its value to you."

That's laying it on the line! No hemming or hawing. No subterfuge. No hiding in the bushes. No double-talk. Just a clear-cut statement: "I want an order and am here to get one."

Usually he did. This ex-preacher carried home $100,000 a year.

Great closers aren't all so speedy about their closes. But all try early in the sale to get the order. Mark your second rule well and use it consistently. It will send you to the bank regularly and frequently.

3. CLOSE ON EVERY RESISTANCE

Strange advice? Wait, it works. That is all that counts, isn't it, a technique that will get you more sales and dollars?

The buyer has just thrown a resistance at you. He has said he isn't going to buy. He doesn't like your product. He doesn't like your firm. He is already loaded up. He is so poor his old aunt in Keokuk has gone to work as a supermarket checker to keep him going. You don't expect him to buy, do you?

Buying is just *exactly* what you expect. When he says no, rush in with a closing action.

Jack Nickerson, a salesperson of a management service, is calling on a buyer twice his age, always a handicap for a youngster. The buyer, Caleb Bush, is a salesperson-baiter. He prides himself on never having been sold. He buys, yes. But buying must always be his idea, never the seller's.

This day, to make confusion more confounded, Bush isn't feeling well. Further, his stocks are down on the exchange. He's in a hurry to get rid of the salesman.

"No sale, son," he says. "I am not interested. I have forgotten more about management than your outfit will ever know. Good-day now."

He turned to other things on his desk.

What does the young salesperson do? He tries for a close.

Jack stands up—that gives him a physical advantage. He smiles, which always helps. He writes out an order, places it in front of the prospect, and says sweetly, "Mr. Bush, your initials will be all I need to get this service started."

"Who said I wanted the service started?" bellows Bush. "Didn't you hear me say I wasn't going to buy?"

"I heard you," says Jack. "I didn't believe it. I don't believe you do. What do you say we get going on this thing at once?"

Caleb Bush signed.

"Do you do that with all your prospects, get orders when they have just told you they aren't going to buy?" Bush asked Nickerson.

"How else? I'll never have the prospect in a more vulnerable position than when he is turning me down."

"How's that?"

"When a boxer throws a punch hard, he throws himself off-balance. The same with a prospect. He's unpoised and his mind temporarily is closed. What better time to go after him for an order?"

Now it won't work every time. It may not work three times out of five. But if you try to close on a resistance and lose, what have you lost? The buyer has already said no. Learn, memorize, practice, and abide by the third rule: close on each resistance.

4. KEEP TRYING

Keep on trying to close, even after the buyer has turned you down, no matter how many times.

You tried for a close and the buyer turned you down. You tried to close on his resistance and he turned you down again. Is all lost? Feel your pulse. If your heart is still beating, keep on trying to close.

Go back into the sale a bit. Build it back up again. Then try for another close. Try on all the closing actions you can think of until he buys—which he is likely to do—or finally gets rid of you for good.

There is hardly anything in selling to match this show of courage. Try and try and try as long as you're in the presence of the prospect.

I baited an old pro salesperson once to see how often he'd try to close before he threw in the towel. I put him off purposely, consciously, unreasonably, but he kept right on doggedly trying to close.

I needed his product for my office. I wanted it anyway, but wanted to see how many times he would come back for more. He tried 16 times.

When all was over, the order signed, I asked him how many more times he would have tried for a close.

"I would have been in there as long as you would have let me—a week if necessary," he said.

That was an old pro talking, recommending the fourth rule of the formula—keep right on trying.

ADD SEVEN KEYS TO FORMULA

When true selling professionals follow this four-point formula, they link it up with time-tested closing techniques.

If one fails, they use another. If that fails, they have another. They are prepared to meet any kind of prospect on his own home-ground and beat him until he buys.

You're going to learn the closing keys—secret and special—in this book. But it's more important to know the formula and be willing to activate it than to know the techniques. Many salespeople have closed volume sales with the crudest of techniques. No salesperson who strayed from the four-point formula made it big.

Does that make this short chapter the most important in the book? Yes.

To their everlasting loss, unfortunately, too many salesfolk won't practice the formula.

A salesperson called on me recently. He had a good product and presented his story well.

"You are certainly sold on what you are selling, and I admire that in a salesperson," I said.

"I am," agreed the salesperson.

"You've sold me on it, but I've been wondering how long it will be before you ask me to buy."

"I was coming to that in a minute," said the salesperson, by now considerably nonplussed.

"Well?" I asked.

"Will you give me an order?"

"Of course I will," I said. "But what took you so long?"

Clearly this salesperson hadn't learned the rules of the four-rule formula. Now you know them all. You're ready for the seven secret closing keys.

YOUR SEVEN SECRET
CLOSING KEYS

10

RUDYARD KIPLING described the
five senses as "five serving men that taught me all I know."
Salespeople use *seven* serving men—seven secret keys that
unlock sales.

Actually, you'll be equipped with an arsenal of closing
keys as powerful as the bandoleers of a helicopter machine
gunner. All are variations of the seven major secrets. Master
and use these seven keys. Once you learn the basics, the
variations come later.

Closing sales is like playing poker. The rules of the game
are simple. Almost everyone can learn how after a few hands.
But no serious player ever so completely masters poker as to
stop trying to learn more—even Amarillo Slim, who frequently
wins the World Series of Poker in Las Vegas. He wins one year
fully aware that someone can knock him off next year—as
sometimes they do.

The rules for closing sales are simple, but no one has ever
mastered the technique enough to stop trying to do it better.

In the chapters ahead, you'll get seven tested keys for closing sales, with examples from the world's most effective salespeople.

Adapt and adopt these techniques in your closing. Each key depends largely upon circumstances and upon two personalities: yours *and* your prospect's. Some techniques won't ever seem natural to you. Some will. Some you may never be able to use effectively. Others you will. You don't have to use them all to upgrade your closing considerably.

Keep as many arrows in your selling quiver as possible. When time and place are right, you will have the equipment to make a difficult sale—any kind of sale. Start by knowing all seven. If you may find one or two of them foreign to your temperament and personality, don't use them. But start with knowledge.

DEVELOP YOUR OWN

George Higbee, outstanding closer, followed a method so individual and so unusual that none of his salesforce could use it—although he tried to teach it to them. It was a stunt that worked for Higbee—an individually-tailored stunt that wasn't transferrable.

Higbee sold insurance. When it was time to close, he uncapped his fountain pen and (with the application blank as a ramp) rolled the uncapped pen toward the prospect.

The prospect, seeing a runaway fountain pen coming toward him, took up the pen in great haste, naturally in his writing hand. There was the prospect, an order blank in front of him, a fountain pen in hand. What was needed to make him sign? Only a few words that the persuasive Higbee always had on tap.

With this peculiar technique Higbee was eminently successful. It was an individual closing technique, based upon a sound principle—the Do Something Key, which you'll read about shortly.

At the opposite pole of this high-pressure trick was Blake Reed, another master salesperson. Reed owned his own business and had salespeople working for him. But he was always the company's best salesperson.

Yet Reed's salesmanship lacked variety. The only closing technique he used was to energetically go from place to place asking for an order. This technique is important—the Ask and Get Key. Most effective salespeople recommend it after other techniques have failed. Yet this one key made Reed quite successful.

These two examples show that temperament—yours and your prospect's—has a great deal to do with the kind of closing technique you use.

If you know all the closing techniques and practice each until you master it, you'll have seven times as much opportunity to close. Don't fall into a rut of using just one closing technique over and over again. Adjust the seven keys to your personality, your products, and your prospects, and more sales will certainly follow.

Here's a preview of the seven secrets of closing sales. Get the overview first and then—chapter by chapter—we'll take up each in detail. (We'll follow this with the special keys but for now—the majors.)

1. The Beyond Any Doubt Key. You close by assuming the prospect is going to buy. You take it for granted the buyer is going to say *Yes*.

2. The Little Question Key. By getting the buyer to decide upon something of secondary importance—such as upholstery color in the automobile, or master bedroom shape in a $30,000 house—you make the buyer tell you he or she is ready to buy.

3. The Do Something Key. Good salesmen and saleswomen follow this rule: physical action is the easiest, surest, quickest way to make the buyer buy. Nine sales in ten should be closed by physical action in some form.

4. The Coming Event Key. This is based upon some impending event that hastens the prospect along in buying. Although it savors of high pressure, it has a legitimate place in the closing ritual of an effective salesperson, as you will see.

5. The Third Party Endorsement Key. Here's narrative selling. You tell stories about other users to illustrate points and bring action. This form of closing—one of the most effective—helps you to make difficult sales otherwise not possible.

6. **The Something for Nothing Key.** You rest your case by introducing a special inducement to buy. This technique is almost perfect if properly used. It appeals to the something-for-nothing weakness in each human being.

7. **The Ask and Get Key.** At certain times, the best selling strategy is asking boldly for the order. This technique, like the other six, must be used carefully, at the right time, and under the right conditions.

Master these seven closing techniques and you'll be equipped to make the difference between $8000 and $80,000 income.

FIT THE TOOL TO THE NEED

The obvious question to ask is: *which* of the seven to use *when* in a given selling situation? Some prospects will not respond to certain techniques. There are various types of prospects. Some are harder to sell than others. Some are amenable to one technique. Others wouldn't respond to that technique under any circumstances.

Take the Coming Event Key. A cogent way to close sales, if properly used on the right prospects. But obviously suspicious-type prospects are offended if you push them toward the sale by mentioning an event that might affect their ability to buy later. On the other hand, the technique will work probably with seven out of ten buyers.

How can you tell which buyers not to try it on? Well, you know that because you make a continuing study of prospects and customers. As you go through a sale, make mental notes of the type of prospect you're talking to. Select one of the seven closing techniques which might cause this prospect to buy. This game of mental gymnastics will pay great dividends.

You can't treat prospects all alike. Scrutinize each one's characteristics (which are bound to surface if you talk long enough) and square those characteristics with the closing technique you think most suitable for a prospect of that temperament.

FIT YOUR PERSONALITY

Not surprisingly, some salespeople do better with one technique than with others. Not all salespeople are so constituted to use all seven techniques with equal skill and effectiveness. Not all salesfolk are versatile enough to be equally skilled with each of the seven.

What you should do is practice, first in your own mind, then on actual prospects, each of these seven techniques a sufficient number of times. Keep it up until you can tell which are most natural and effective for your personality.

Then develop those as much as you can. You'll probably have a favorite. But don't neglect the others because one happens to come easier. When a buyer doesn't respond to your pet technique, you'll need other arrows in your quiver.

When the moment to close arrives, choose the closing technique most appropriate. This is where judgment comes in. No one can tell you much more than this. It all comes down to a judgment based on sufficient practice.

If you should misjudge your prospect, don't give the sale up as a lost cause. Go back. Rebuild. Try to close again, this time using a different technique.

Often a prospect impervious to your best attempts one way will be a quick take on another technique. Don't be Johnny-One-Note. The more techniques you master, the more opportunities you'll have for closing more sales.

THE RIGHT KEY

Selecting the right key need not concern you too much. Subconsciously you'll tend to pick the right one—once you know them all well. Use depends on belief in a certain key, personality, and, yes, size.

A 250-pound former football tackle selling steel to industry will probably use a different approach from a 97-pound cosmetics saleswoman. He may prefer a more "physical" approach. She may prefer to use finesse and charm. Yet both can be effective closers.

Certain keys make more sense to some than to others. Red Motley usually selected the Friendly Third Party Key because telling stories came naturally to him. He told what someone had done, what results they gained. He closed sales that way.

W.N. Blayney, a rough-finished fellow, merely used the Ask and Get Key. It was natural to him. He couldn't tell stories like Red Motley. He was a digger and he capitalized on his talents that way.

Expect to have a favorite key, but study and use them all, as you need them. Now it's time to dig into each chapter so you'll be prepared in depth.

THE
BEYOND ANY DOUBT
KEY

11

THE MARQUEE ON THE one-man show said *Banjo Dancing*. A critic was quoted: "Fascinating Americana." Yet as people filed into the off-Broadway theatre, they wondered. After all, in a one-man show, everything depends on the lone performer's charisma. But once Stephen Wade ambled up from the *back* of the auditorium, the audience became enslaved.

After a rousing opening singing and playing the five-string banjo, Wade pulled out a ballpoint pen. He said to a man sitting in the front row:

"Now you're ready to buy this pen. Only 25 cents." The man paid his quarter and took the pen.

"Never lose a chance to sell customers with money in their hands," Wade chanted.

He ran to the stage and grabbed two handfuls of pens.

"These pens write on both sides of the paper," he said and collected for ten more.

He ran up and down the aisles.

"These pens write in any language," he said and sold 20 more.

125

The audience was rabid. People stood up, money in hand, yelling:

"Here! Take mine! I want one!"

After selling 40 pens for a quarter each, Wade ran out of product—and went on with the show.

"That act—patterned on the performance of an actual pen salesperson—is also part of Americana," said Wade. "In this country, if you assume people are going to buy, and then ask them right, they *do* buy."

Here's an outstanding demonstration of the *Beyond Any Doubt Key*. Wade never had any doubt that his audience would buy. (Afterward, each purchaser found he'd bought an advertising specialty pen promoting *Banjo Dancing*—the kind of premium promoters often provide free). Because the audience sensed Wade *knew* they'd buy, they bought—en masse.

Now watch a full-time professional salesperson use the same technique. Bill Decker sells furnishings to hotels, motels, dormitories, and other institutions. This exacting business requires top salesmanship.

Bill Decker is a master. In his field, you cannot rush a prospect off his feet, you must use slow sell, soft sell—but you must close hard.

In reaching for a $150,000 order for furnishing and equipping a new motel, Decker has to make two sales—to

- The architect or backer
- The motel operator

The second buyer is always involved. Usually he is an architect. Sometimes it's the interior decorator. It may be the financier (to have money to start with, you know he's a shrewd buyer).

Decker goes to the secondary buyer first. He uses the first key—Beyond Any Doubt. He assumes his furnishings and equipment are what the buyer wants. No doubt about it. He paints word pictures of what the motel will be like with these installations.

"It will be wonderful to have long-lasting furnishings like this from the start!" he says enthusiastically. "You do want that appearance and quality, don't you?"

"Sounds good," the secondary says.

Sale Number One is thus made. Then Bill approaches the motel operator, armed with the approval of the designer or financier. Of course he tells Secondary he's seeking to close Primary.

He plays both ends against the middle. Behind it is the simplest of all closing keys: he assumes he'll get the order. It's one of the most interesting and successful closing techniques: The Beyond Any Doubt Key.

EXPECT TO SELL

The philosophy of this technique is assumption. You take the sale for granted. You assume there's no thought in the buyer's head except signing up for your product or service.

When you learned about the buyer's emotional state, you discovered his mental condition at closing is not normal. This means you must be absolute in everything you say and do—never doubtful. Doubt, waver, question, wander, quibble, and inquire—and so will the buyer. Be positive, dogmatic, absolute, and confident, and you'll build like qualities in his or her mind—and close.

To use Beyond Any Doubt, you sweep the buyer forward by holding that assumption strongly in your mind and in front of the buyer's eyes.

You're sitting in the prospect's office. You sense he's getting ready for a close. The Beyond Any Doubt Key fits in naturally with the conditions. You say: "May I use this phone for a minute? I want to call the office and tell them how you want this handled." The buyer says: "Certainly." That's your answer: you've got the order.

Wasn't that simple, natural, easy, and satisfactory? You merely assumed he was going to buy, and pushed forward on that assumption. He bought. But perhaps he wouldn't have bought if an unskilled salesperson had asked him for his order.

The great secret of this technique is the absolute and undoubting assumption in your mind that you're going to sell and that the buyer's going to buy. You must honestly feel it isn't a question of *whether*. You *know* he's going to buy. Of that you are positive. You assume it's merely a question of getting together on a few details such as terms and delivery. The only question really is *when*.

WHEN, NOT IF

The word *when* is a magic word in forcing the close. Even unspoken the word *when* is useful. If your customer wants what you are selling, there's almost certainly a definite time *when* she wants it. Get her to center on that question of time, and you force a decision—without either of you being aware of any forcing.

Suppose you're showing clothes to a retail customer. She likes the coat but is indecisive. You say:

"Let me see. You want this garment by next Sunday at the latest. This is Friday. We can manage that nicely. We can get delivery Saturday morning."

You do not need to ask *if* she'll buy. You assume she will. Unless there are definite obstacles to prevent it (such as inability to pay) you'll close the sale then and there. The Beyond Any Doubt Key often makes buying easier than *not* buying.

To vary your closing, ask her: "How soon *must* you have this suit?"

You assume you're going to get it. You proceed in a serene, self-confident way. Act as if you *already* have it.

LEAD YOUR CUSTOMER

The assumption that the prospect is going to buy must come from you. It must be in *your* mind *first*, inextricably bound up in your opinion of yourself as a professional salesperson. It must be firmly in *your* mind before it can be transmitted to the customer's mind.

If you hesitate, so will the customer. If you have doubts or qualms, doubts or qualms will fill her mind. You must be self-assured, positive, forceful. Say nothing or do nothing not predicated on the absolute belief that the sale is just as good as made.

A sales counselor was looking at an expensive Manhattan office space. The rental agent knew his business. He showed one suite after another, never assuming for a moment that the prospect wasn't going to lease. The only question in his mind: *which* offices would suit the prospect best?

After explaining the different offices, the rental salesperson judged closing time had arrived. He deftly used the Beyond Any Doubt Key.

He led the prospect into one suite overlooking the Hudson, and asked:

"Do you like the view of the Hudson River?"

The prospect said, yes, he did.

Then the salesperson took him to the other side of the building and asked him if he liked the skyline view.

"Very much," the counselor responded.

"Which view do you like better?"

The prospect thought. Then he said: "You can't beat the river."

"That's the office you want, of course," said the salesperson—and the deal was closed.

The prospect didn't have a chance to escape.

You'll develop many ways to use Beyond Any Doubt in your own selling. This technique is valuable because (1) it's so useful in so many different situations and (2) because it's so safe. You cause no offense by mildly assuming the prospect will buy. You apply no pressure. Quietly and gently you lead him to a decision, having arrived at that decision in your own mind first.

Samuel Horowitz, one of the greatest salesmen of his generation, was a rich contractor. When he started talking to Frank W. Woolworth about building the Woolworth Building in New York, he ran into all sorts of difficulties and competitive problems.

Woolworth was befuddled and undecided. He didn't even know whether he wanted to build that building he'd dreamed about for years. Could supersalesmanship make him buy?

Super persuasion was mother's milk for Sam. After another fruitless call at Woolworth's office (the same evasiveness and indecision) Horowitz, with a slight show of resentment, rose, extended his hand, and said testily:

"I am going to tell you something, Mr. Woolworth. You are going to build the largest building in the world, and I am going to build it for you. Good morning."

He walked out.

Several months later when work had started on the building, Woolworth said to this master salesman:

"Do you remember the morning you told me I was going to build the largest building in the world and you were going to build it for me?"

"Yes."

"Well, I never was able to get that out of my mind."

Of course, you don't sell million-dollar units. But use the closing technique just the same.

The same quality of assumption, the same feeling of self-confidence, the same serenity and belief that sold the Woolworth Building will help close sales for you, whether for a few dollars or a few million dollars.

WE'VE GOT TO GO

Sometimes military stories illustrate the Beyond Any Doubt Key. Old Amos, a discharged British Army sergeant, was too valuable to leave on retirement when war started again. But the recruiters couldn't get him to go back into the service. The local magistrate talked to him, told him it was his duty to enlist. Nothing doing. His wife and sons worked on him. He was adamant.

Other influential people appealed to patriotism, to pride, to obligation to country. They were all whipped. This was one war, old Amos said, they'd have to fight without him.

At length, his old company commander said: "I believe I can get Amos to enlist. Let me try."

"You'll fail," the recruiter said. "We all tried. We failed."

"Just the same, I'm going to talk to him."

He went to Amos' retirement cottage and talked about old times. The captain didn't appeal to patriotism, duty, self-sacrifice.

"Do you remember the time we bogged down there at Vimy Ridge, and how hot they made it for us?" he asked Amos.

"Very well I do."

"And do you remember the mud, and the rats?"

"No man can forget that!" responded old Amos.

They talked like this for maybe ten minutes. Then the officer, after a long silence, arose and said:

"Well, Amos, we're in it again and I guess we've got to go."

Amos arose and said: "Yes, sir. We're in it again," and went down to the recruiting office and reenlisted.

Credit the Beyond Any Doubt Key with another sale!

E.F. Gregory, prominent in health and accident insurance, uses this key almost to exclusion of every other closing technique. Gregory doesn't ask his prospect for name, address, age, and so forth. He asks: "Did you ever have an operation?"

"Yes. Ten years ago."

Gregory writes that information on the application blank. He put it on the desk in front of him. Seeing Gregory write on the blanks makes the prospect come to life in a hurry:

"Hey, I didn't say I was going to take the policy."

Gregory's calm reply: "I know you didn't. Right now, as I look at you and talk to you, I see no reason why you couldn't get it. But our underwriting department is pretty fussy. After we have run through this health chart, I can probably tell you whether you can get it or not."

By this time the prospect has come to see that he *does* want the insurance.

See how safely you can close sales with the Beyond Any Doubt Key?

TRY A BIGGER ORDER

A widely-practiced variation on this technique is to ask for more than you expect. A man who wants to borrow $25 asks for $50. In self-defense, the friend says he can't possibly let him have $50, but would $25 help?

Former Vice-President Tom Marshall of Indiana (famed for "what this country needs is a good five-cent cigar") concluded the best way to get an appropriation approved in Congress was to ask for twice as much. Congress, thinking itself shrewd and economical, cut the budget in half—to exactly the amount Marshall wanted.

In selling, outline a buying plan more ambitious than you think the prospect can or will approve. Assume he or she needs the larger amount. If the prospect takes it, wonderful. Chances are he'll suggest a compromise, a smaller amount you've privately decided you'd be happy to get.

James Morris, an office equipment salesman, racked up an extraordinary success record in a hard field by suggesting that the customer put a number of machines on trial—a far greater number than the prospect can use. Cutting down the order distracts the prospect's mind. No longer is he concerned about whether to try the machines in the first place—only about the correct number to try. This try-a-larger-number tack has made Morris the leader in his company for many years.

ASKING MORE—EXPECTING MORE

Charles Mandel, top-flight magazine space salesman, takes the ask-more plan one step further: he asks for more and expects to get it *all*. In many cases, he gets more, too.

"If a guy wants to buy a page, then my job is to sell him two," Mandel says. "A salesman's job is to maximize the buy. When I call on an advertiser who wants to buy a page, I know my job is to convince him to buy 12 pages."

Mandel, whose selling expertise pushed him up the ladder to his current post as publisher of *Science Digest*, tells his salesforce to turn a *maybe* to a *yes*—a 2-page buyer to 4 pages, a 4-page buyer to 12 pages.

"Recently, one of my salesmen walked in with a 12-page schedule," Mandel said. "He told me how wonderful the advertiser is and how much he loved the magazine. I said, 'Terrific, let's go back and see him.' My salesman thought I'd blow the whole deal. I asked the buyer why he bought 12 pages. He had co-op money he had to spend before Christmas. I said: 'Why don't you buy 36 pages?' The order went from 12 pages to 36 pages.

"Actually, when the advertiser says he wants 12 pages, the salesman's job is just beginning. His problem: to get the advertiser from 12 to 13 pages. After all, the buyer bought 12 *on his own!*"

Mandel believes *why* is the key question.

Charles Mandel asks for more, expects to get it, and almost always does. This is *Beyond Any Doubt*—up one power.

THE POWER OF INDIRECTION

Suggestion is perhaps the most powerful force in human affairs. Be indirect. Suggest, never state. Imply, don't declare.

Many salespeople use the indirect method to vast profit. Psychologists tell us seven out of ten people are suggestible.

"You will want this suit to wear to the Friday meeting won't you?" you ask. "Yes," says the prospect.

"Will this color go better with your drapes than the other?" "I think it will."

Do you think three dozen will do as a starter?" "Yes."

So it goes, with you making suggestions, your prospect agreeing with them.

The happiest thing about the indirect question is that you are very seldom turned down. Ask a person directly to buy and he or she can say no. But it won't happen often when you use the indirect question.

THE MEHDI STORY

Mehdi Fakharzadeh*, one of selling's major success stories, is a prime user of Beyond Any Doubt. Yet he is probably the most unlikely salesman extant. In 1948, Mehdi came to the U.S. from the Middle East. He had to learn English. He started as sales trainee for Metropolitan Life. He also had to learn insurance and selling. All the odds were against him.

Today he's the top producer on MetLife's 25,000-plus salesforce. Sales commissions have made him a millionaire.

---

*Reprinted with permission from "Mehdi: Nothing Is Impossible", published by Farnsworth Publishing Company, Inc., Copyright, 1978.

Mehdi always assumes each prospect will buy. Most do. He never doubts his ability to sell—or the prospect's ability to buy. Mehdi sold nine Key Man insurance plans to a prominent New Jersey utility consulting firm. The head man explained why:

"He was very business-like. He didn't come on strong. Direct opposite of the high-pressure salesman. He spoke factually. He quoted figures. After he presented his case, the only sensible thing to do was to buy. We did."

Mehdi's Beyond-Any-Doubt presentations to business owners appeal primarily to reason. Listen as Mehdi discusses Key Person insurance with partners Tom and Tony:

> Tom, what would happen to this business if (Mehdi never suggests the person he's talking to will die) your partner Tony dies? The loss of a key person can hurt a company more than almost any other tragedy. It's one of the major reasons companies fail. I have a plan that can protect your company.
>
> I don't know if we can afford it.
>
> I recommend insuring you and Tony at $300,000 each. If your partner dies, my company will pay the money tax-free.
>
> That sounds like too much insurance coverage.
>
> Is it? You and Tony together account for $6 million in sales each year. What do you earn on each dollar of sales?
>
> Last year about five cents on every dollar.
>
> So there you are. Five percent of $6 million is $300,000. A business policy will insure your profits. But, Tom, that's not all. It will make it easier for your company to borrow money.
>
> How's that?
>
> Consider. What's a bank's concern in loaning money?
>
> Getting the money back, of course.
>
> Well, if Tony dies, your business might fail since both of you together account for $6 million in sales. You could go bankrupt. But my plan insures your company's capability of paying back a major loan.
>
> And it will cost how much?
>
> Practically nothing. It's like transferring money from one pocket to another. The money you transfer to my plan

will always be available to you. Through the first 12 to 13 years of the plan the difference between your annual outlays and the amount available to you is about two years' worth of outlays. After that, more money becomes available to you.

So how much do I give you each year?

Depending on your age, about two-and-one half to three percent of your coverage.

That's about $12,000! Do you know how much return on investment I can get on $12,000 in my business? Fifty percent!

I know you're a very good businessman and can earn this rate of return. If your company faces an emergency, the insurance company will loan you back all the money you pay in minus two years during the first 12 to 13 years. They will charge you only five percent. And since the interest rate is tax deductible, your loan meets certain requirements, it costs you only two-and-one half percent.

But as I borrow money, I have less coverage, right?

That's certainly true—which is why it is important to pay back policy loans as soon as you can. But at least until the loan is repaid I can add a clause that the cash value of the plan is guaranteed. We request that part of your dividends purchase one-year term insurance equal to the amount of cash value. So you see, my plan helps protect your company's profits in case either you or Tony dies.

Your company gets tax-free money equal to your profit contribution. This profit protection, in turn, helps bolster your credit rating. Further, the money you pay into the plan is still available if your company should need it for emergencies or any other reason. You win all the way around.

Did you ever see the slightest doubt in Mehdi's mind that Tom was going to buy? You didn't? Either did Tom or Tony when Mehdi talked to each one separately.

No wonder Mehdi clients say: After Mehdi's finished, there's only one thing you can do—buy.

The first closing key you've learned—Beyond Any Doubt—is useful and effective, the simplest to apply, the safest to use. Often you'll surprise yourself by getting business you had decided was impossible. Assume the prospect will buy, that he can't help buying, and that you are going to make the sale. Then proceed as if settling a few questions of detail was the only thing left to do. Often it *is*.

THE LITTLE
QUESTION KEY

12

CLOSING SALES isn't ever a simple either-or proposition. If you force the buyer to give you a *yes* or *no*, it'll often be a *no*.

If you lead the buyer gently, by giving him or her easy, safe questions to answer, the buyer will often tell you, in effect, that he or she will buy.

This is the psychological basis for the Little Question Key to closing sales.

Don't force the buyer into a corner and demand an answer to a major question. Give him or her a simple little question relating to what you are selling. In answering, he or she is buying.

THE MONOGRAM CONNECTION

On Long Island, Bright Harrow broke all records selling a $20,000 luxury car. His extraordinary closing skill won him the business. Once he talked to a customer and built the customer's interest, it was all over but the check signing. This salesperson landed three out of five deals—the talk of the industry.

From Detroit came a corporate sales expert to learn how Harrow did it, so he could teach salespeople in other cities. The Detroiter worked with Harrow for a week, watched him sell, kept tabs on everything. The corporate expert concluded that Harrow was strongest in the spot most other salesmen are weakest—in the close.

Harrow had worked out a very effective closing technique. It was simple, and it was natural, but apparently it was indomitable. It worked on the old, it worked on the young. It worked on men or women. It worked on the arrogant as well as on the meek.

Here's what he did. He knew his car, so of course he'd explain its plus points, intrigue his customer, appeal to the ego—all sure-fire selling tactics. Then when closing time came, he introduced the closing art. He was extremely nonchalant about the whole business, nonchalant but not indifferent. He brought out a little book of gold monograms, the kind you see on doors of swanky expensive cars. He placed them in front of the customer.

"Now let us decide which form of monogram you like," he would say.

Mind you, the customer hadn't said anything about buying the car, hadn't even indicated he was more than interested in it, hadn't said he was convinced. No matter. Harrow talked engagingly about the monograms. He discussed his choice and asked the customer if he would like the same style. No? The customer had always fancied Old English type in a car monogram.

"Pretty hard to read, isn't it?" Harrow suggested. Yes, harder to read than Roman type. True enough. But class—it had class, didn't he think? This Harrow would admit. The discussion of monograms went on, perhaps for five minutes or longer. The customer at length decided upon the very best monogram.

And in deciding upon the monograms, he had agreed to buy, and pay for, a $20,000 automobile!

Harrow was using the Little Question Closing Key.

A little question is merely a question pertaining to some secondary or subordinate phase of the product or sale. Yet, in answering that question, the buyer gives you permission to enter his or her order.

NAIL-DOWN-DETAIL-QUESTION

The Little Question assumes that the sale is already made and that you are simply clearing up a few final details.

The handbag saleswoman approaches the prospect examining a purse and says, "What a lovely purse! It matches your shoes perfectly. Would you like to take it with you or shall we send it to your home?" If the prospect has not yet decided to buy, no harm done. The saleswoman simply helps her find a purse more to her liking.

A real estate salesperson, after showing a prospect a $70,000 house, says, "Mr. and Mrs. Rockland, I know you will be delighted with this fine home. How would your name appear on the mailbox?" Again, the prospects' decision to buy is assumed. Instead of asking them, "Do you want to buy this $70,000 home?" the salesperson suggests a very small decision. If the prospects respond by saying, "Oh, 'The Rocklands' will be fine," they've agreed to buy the $70,000 house.

The subordinate question skips over the primary question—which always is: "Are you going to buy this from me?" It ignores that question entirely. It *assumes* the buyer is going to buy. It poses a question on an unimportant point or detail.

Yet when the customer answers that unimportant question, he has given, without being aware of it, his consent to buy.

The Little Question Key is the smoothest, most effective way to close. It can't possibly cause offense. If the customer isn't ready to buy, she merely thinks you *really are* asking her about details. She doesn't suspect you're turning on the heat. If she *is* ready to buy, she accepts the question as a matter of course, and buys, believing she made up her mind and that you didn't have anything to do with it!

Earlier you learned to try to close just as soon as possible. You'll recall that questions are the ideal way to practice the experimental close. Now you will understand why.

You say to a buyer: "Do you prefer the tan or the blue suit?"

He answers he prefers the blue, which is the same as saying: "I will take the blue suit."

Bill Tobin says: Give the customer a choice of two yeses! "Do you like the blue or white color?" (Sell one or the other—or both!) "Would $10,000 be too much?" (Sell a $5,000 article instead!) Any answer is a buying commitment.

If he isn't ready to answer or to buy, he will tell you there are certain points he'd like cleared up. Or he may ask to see other suits. Whichever way, you haven't lost a thing—but have gained a great deal—by asking the question.

If unleashing a force this powerful, be aware of certain dangers. If you fail to handle the question deftly, the prospect will get the idea you're giving him the rush act. Then of course, the buyer will tell you he'll do his own deciding, thank you. But if you're gentle enough and shrewd enough in presenting the right question, he won't know *you're* doing the deciding.

The Little Question Key, used often and in the right way, will win sales from prospects who cannot be influenced by any other kind of closing technique.

ASSUMPTIVE CLOSING

Robert Connolly tacks the Little Question on his assumptive close. It works.

In using this technique, you assume your prospect has made the purchase decision. You proceed by explaining the action you are planning to take.

When the prospect has not yet reached a positive decision, the assumptive close will draw him toward a buying decision, or at least cause him to declare himself. By using the assumptive close, you at least find out where you stand and you often get the order.

Your prospect seems to feel that one piece of property is what he wants. But he seems inert, unable to make a decision. Perhaps he is stalling. You try the assumptive close.

"Mr. Jones, I can see you feel strongly toward the (blank) residence, and that it fills your needs very well. Tell you what we'll do. We'll submit an offer at $1,000 below the asking price and see how much we can save for you. Would it be more comfortable to do the paper work at my office or here?"

Never be afraid to add the Little Question to the assumptive close. If you speak with sincerity and concern for your prospect's interests, assumptive closing can only help you. Many prospects appreciate your assistance in their buying decision.

"At worst, your prospect will let you know where he stands so you can further help him toward his purchase," Connolly says. "Always remember, he wants to buy, to say yes, to solve his buying problem. Any assistance you can offer, properly rendered in terms of your prospect's interest, will be of value to you both."

THE CHOICE

Lola Peterson, a Chicago millinery saleswoman, led her department three years running. Her secret: she sold the Lookers. A Looker says frankly he or she is "just looking" and most retail salespeople dislike him or her intensely.

But to a capable and skilled salesperson, The Looker is a source of sales. Lola Peterson perceived that. She used the Little Question Key. It almost always worked.

When she has The Looker at a closing point, Peterson merely asks: "Would you like to wear this hat, or shall I send it to your home?" There is nothing original about this. But using it consistently built a distinguished sales record.

A real estate subdivider sold $300,000 worth of lots in a single year. This man is expert on the close. His closing question: "Do you want this lot registered in your own or your wife's name?"

The best salesman I have ever heard introduced his question so gently and adroitly the prospect couldn't possibly resent it. He was selling a very intricate and expensive installation. His presentation lasted two hours. He appeared to have no eagerness whatever to close. He acted in a leisurely, friendly way.

When he judged the time had come, he merely said, very quietly and matter-of-factly: "Shall I ship by freight or truck?" See how easy to order, merely by making a secondary choice about transportation? The prospect made the choice and the sale was closed without fuss or worry or uncertainty.

QUERYING HESITATORS

Hubert Bermont tells about using the Little Question in a different way—by asking why the customer is hesitating.

At one point, I was losing sales I couldn't afford to lose. I reached excellent rapport with prospects. They seemed to trust me and like my merchandise and prices. But I faced indecision I couldn't overcome.

"I have to talk it over with my wife."

"Let me go home and think about it."

"I'll definitely call you tomorrow." I just couldn't close those sales. So I set up a meeting with a salesperson earning $75,000 a year in commissions. I explained my plight. He said something I never forgot:

"As long as you are going to strike out anyhow, why don't you strike out swinging?"

I thought I *was* swinging.

"Why don't you simply ask the customers why you're not closing the sale?" he suggested.

"Since they like you, since they like the merchandise and since they like the prices ... instead of asking me why they are walking out without buying, why not ask them? You're forgetting the most crucial, final step. You are forgetting to ask for the order!"

I tried that. I asked the very next customer who faltered why he was hesitating. He looked puzzled and then said:

"I really don't know why. I have no reason. Write it up. I'll buy it now."

This simple question closed eight out of ten such prospective sales. By simply swinging, I didn't strike out half as often.

PLAYING THE MINOR LEAGUE

Always give customers a minor (never a major) choice. Be happy with a *small* question. Remember the advice of theatre pioneer Stanislavsky: "There are no small parts, only small actors." There's no end to possibilities. It's versatile, fascinating, strong and safe, and simple.

No matter what you're selling, no matter whom you sell to, whether you're big-ticket or discount, the Little Question is one of the most useful closing secrets you'll ever learn.

Assume the prospect will buy. When the time comes to close, merely ask a question about something entirely secondary—and thus leave the buyer, not with the choice of buying or not buying, but with a very minor subordinate matter to decide.

The buyer usually won't hesitate about making a minor choice. Yet if you were to ask for a major choice, your buyer could shy off, and you would miss the order.

The Little Question brings big sales results, over and over again.

THE DO SOMETHING

KEY

13

suggests that you buy a set of books. On the colorful folder is a blank space. In the envelope are two gummed stamps.

"Paste down your stamp indicating your choice of bindings and rush it back to us," the copy explains.

Now why the stamp? Why not merely send back the order? Because, for a very good reason, people are more positively inclined to buy when they *Do Something*. You sell more books when you give the prospect the option of pasting down the stamp, experts say.

The *why* of it may mystify gurus of mail-order. But the seasoned salesperson understands it very well in daily practice. People respond to the Do Something Key. It closes thousands of sales every day.

Court French was right in the middle of his presentation. He had Jon Beacham's attention. Things were going well. Then French stood up, crossed over to Beacham's desk, and asked:

"May I use your phone?"

"Of course," said Jon Beacham.

French smiled.

"I just want to make sure that we have enough of this product to take care of your needs," he explained. "I'd hate to see you disappointed after we have gone this far."

The prospect didn't stop him from calling, so French assumed the sale was closed. And it was.

French was using the Do Something Key. The basis of this key is to start to do something which implies consent. Unless the buyer stops you, you've closed the sale. It is a whopper of a closing key. Master and use it.

One manufacturer hit upon a closing plan using the Do Something Key that increased sales 28 percent in one year. He sent each of his retailers a huge blue pencil. In a personal letter, he asked retailers to follow a simple routine in talking to a prospect about his product.

The blue pencil, the physical basis for closing sales, proved matchless. Wherever used, in large cities or in hamlets, in large stores or in crossroads, it worked. I doubt if anything in the history of American retailing has ever made such sales.

Here's how it worked.

The product was an expensive musical instrument. Use of the blue pencil exemplified the principle of physical action to close sales.

After the salesman had demonstrated the instrument, he stepped toward the prospect and offered the large blue pencil saying:

"Suppose you take this and initial the inside of the cabinet?"

"What for?" the prospect asked, puzzled.

"It's your personal selection. The one you pick is the one you get."

"But I was just looking," objected the customer.

The salesman agreed: "Certainly. I understand. But there is only one question to decide: does this wonderful instrument give you all that the ear could want in music? If it does, you want it. Now if you will take the pencil and initial the instrument, I'll have it up to your house so you can play it before dinner."

There's some pretty strong salesmanship here. A powerful force was working in favor of getting the customer's initials inside the cabinet. In the majority of cases, when the salesman got as far as offering the blue pencil to the customer, he got the order.

USE ACTIONS

Actually, of course, the plan was something more than a blue pencil. The pencil was merely a symbol, the equipment for putting physical-action-in-closing sales into operation.

A secret of all great closers is that they *do* something as well as *say* something. In selling, as in life, actions speak the loudest. By using action in your close, you can bring sales to a close where mere words will fail.

Here's a sound and workable selling principle: start something which the customer will have to stop to avoid giving tacit consent to buy.

A saleswoman, talking to a prospect, senses it's time to close. She decides on physical action.

She brought out the order blank earlier in the interview, so doesn't shock the prospect by flashing it now. The order blank is on the counter between them. She begins to write her order as she verbally outlines it, as if talking to herself.

"You'll want so many dozen of such and such a number," she says, writing that down. "And so much of this," as she writes that down also.

She keeps her eyes glued to the pad. She doesn't look at the buyer. To avoid placing that order, the buyer will have to do something right away. He will have to interrupt. He will have to tell the saleswoman she's premature. Not all buyers have the courage to stop the action, even though they may not be fully determined to buy when you start writing the order.

Thus: most buyers will go ahead and let you write the order—and will sign it—because of the peculiar fascination physical action exerts on the human mind.

Remember the insurance salesman who started a fountain pen rolling toward his prospect? Success of this unusual form of physical action shows the power in this technique if used in the proper way.

Theatrical directors know the power of actions in influencing audiences. If you spend much time around the theatre, you soon know action is even more important than the dialogue. It's also true in selling, where the actions of the salesperson, especially in bringing about the close, can be more persuasive and more powerful than words.

SAFETY SWITCH

Harold Jordan used the Do Something Key to build a multimillion-dollar enterprise in Detroit. He sells safety switches, accepted these days by every industrialist. But when he started, no one knew what a safety switch was, and no one cared. Pioneering of the hardest possible kind was required.

When Jordan took over, he was the entire salesforce, and there were no sales. He tried talking to prospects about the necessity for switches. Nothing. So he evolved a selling process built entirely around Do Something.

It made sales. As he added salespeople, he taught them how to use it. In a few months, the business had grown beyond his projections for the first five years. Eventually it became world-wide.

Here's how it worked. The salesman entered the prospect's office, put a sample on the prospect's desk, and said: "Pull the handle." That physical action started the process. Nine in ten by count pulled the handle.

"You see," said the salesman, "no flash, no danger of fire, no chance for a man to be electrocuted when he pulls that switch." Then he added:

"What kind of safety switches are you now using in your plant?"

"Not any," the prospect said.

The salesman registered astonishment. "What? Not using any safety switches in your plant?"

"No. We've been operating for ten years and haven't had an accident."

Meanwhile the salesman was pulling the lever of the switch. He pushed the sample over where the prospect could touch it. The majority of prospects pulled it once or twice. It was the natural thing to do.

The salesman continued: "Carrying any fire insurance?"

"Certainly."

"How long have you been carrying it?"

"Ten years."

"Ever had a fire?"

"No."

"Why don't you quit carrying insurance?"

"Why, we may have a fire any time and we want to be protected!"

"That's just it. You're also liable to have a switch accident today, and one accident will cost more than equipping your entire plant with safety switches."

Closing time. The salesman, with the order book non-chalantly on the desk beside the sample, picked it up and inquired: "How many 30-amp open-knife switches do you have in the plant?"

If the prospect knew, he would give the information. If he didn't know (usually the case) the salesman said: "Call in your electrician, will you, Mr. Sutton? I'll go through the plant with him and make a count of the switches."

After returning from the inspection, he had the order written up. He casually handed the pencil to the prospect. "Just your name at the bottom, please."

By actual count, nine prospects out of ten invited to sign *did*. If they did not sign, the salesman would return in 30 days and go through the same routine, using the already-filled-out order blank as his presentation. Again, only one out of ten asked to sign failed to sign.

Eventually that firm sold practically all its prospects. The reason: the power of the Do Something Key.

EXPENDABLE ORDER BLANKS

The Do Something physical action can vary from sliding the fountain pen toward the buyer's lap to asking him to initial the inside of a cabinet to putting his name on an order blank. But the principle remains the same: start an action that will result in a sale unless the buyer puts an actual stop to it. Use of Do Something around an order blank is a universal selling custom.

Every morning Ned Sterling goes through the same ritual. With a list of calls in front of him, Sterling carefully writes in the name and address of each prospect on an order blank.

"You're wasting order blanks," his boss reminds him, pleasantly.

"Aren't they cheap?"

"We'll print as many as you need, Ned," says the boss.

When Sterling makes a call, he puts the order blank, with the prospect's name on it, right in front of his nose.

"Let him get used to seeing it," Sterling says.

He makes his presentation, then he fills in the order blank, sometimes over the prospect's protest. He pushes the order blank to the prospect and admonishes him: "Just initial here, please."

There is something mighty fundamental about this—make it easy to buy, hard not to.

The only thing you have to lose in writing it up beforehand is an order blank (which, as Ned Sterling points out, is cheap).

Another firm, experimenting with the fill-out-in-advance plan, found 80 percent of prospects, confronted with their name on an order blank, signed.

Always carry an order blank filled in with your prospect's name and address. What do you have to lose?

SIDE OF COTTAGE CHEESE

Sometimes the Do Something Key can take strange forms. Gary Fink, a champion insurance agent, once sent this letter to a prospect:

Dear Dale:
As per your request, I'm using this means of summarizing our luncheon meeting of the first of July at the

Athletic Club. To the best of my recollection, you had an egg-salad sandwich on pumpernickel with a side of cottage cheese and skim milk, and I ordered a diet burger with cole slaw and two Tabs with lime.

If you have any questions or want any further information, please feel free to contact me at your convenience.

Gary

Gary Fink makes more than $150,000 a year selling insurance in Minneapolis. He believes in the Do Something Key.

THE GLASS OF WATER

Bruce Alexander, ace California real estate salesperson (in a state full of formidable competitors), applies the Do Something Key with all the finesse of a seasoned actor.

After a negotiation session with the house seller, he arrives at Prospective Buyers' House, his tie askew, his hair awry. The buyers, of course, are eagerly awaiting word of Seller's reaction to their latest offer.

When Mr. or Mrs. Prospective Buyer opens the door, Alexander rushes in, rolls his eyes, holds his head and says: "Quick, I've got to have a glass of water!"

The couple rush to the kitchen, fearing some health calamity. He gulps the water, sits, closes his eyes. The pause is dramatic. Slowly he looks up.

"In the last ten years, I've never had a negotiating session like that," he says. "I'm really off the wall. But I held out for you. And believe me, this is the final offer he's going to make. I just hope I'll recover."

The final offer, of course, is still more than Prospects wanted to pay. But by now, they are convinced that only the superhuman effort of a superachiever arranged it. In many cases, they buy then and there. Do Something wins again.

TREAT SIGNING AS DETAIL

The reason salespeople are afraid of order blanks is because they're afraid the customer will be afraid.

The way to treat an order blank is to get it out in front of the customer as early in the sale as possible. This way the buyer gets used to it, and when the closing times comes, it won't shock. Be nonchalant about the blank, never make an issue of it. Treat it naturally as a mere detail.

When you present the blank, make it difficult for the buyer to catch your eye. Look down at the form. Be busy writing. This is a rare selling moment when you *don't* want eye contact. If you look up, the buyer may tell you she isn't quite ready to buy, she wants to think it over. But if you keep looking at the blank and writing, the buyer will have to stop you from doing both to keep from giving you an order.

After the order is filled in, pass it along "to check, Ms. Buyer." At the same time, pass the pen, quietly suggesting that she put her name "right on that line, please." Do it all in the same quiet, nonchalant manner. Because of that highly sensitized abnormal way the buyer thinks at closing time, you don't want to run the risk of driving the order away.

ROCK-BOTTOM PRICE

Penn Glade, a successful salesman in his industry, always makes it a point (after he's pushed the order blank over to the customer) to ask for the blank back and reread it.

"I'm wondering if the price on item three is the price you ought to have," Glade explains. "A buyer as important to us as you are must have the best offer we can make. Yes, that's right, our rockbottom price."

Just as casually as he originally pushed the blank toward the buyer, he pushes it back for the buyer to sign.

"It's the best way in the world to get a buyer to sign an order," Glade says. "It makes him more eager to have it back. Very seldom does a customer fail to sign when he gets the blank back the second time. Besides, my scanning the blank to see if there's any mistake develops confidence."

Use the Do Something Key. You'll find a useful workhorse in closing. It's the action step when your customer is undecided, when *doing* something rather than *saying* something will close the sale.

THE COMING EVENT
KEY

14

IN THIS inflationary era, what better argument than telling a prospect the price will be higher tomorrow? He's sure it will be, so he buys now to avoid paying more later. That prices will rise is a statement unchallenged today.

Using rising prices to close is part of the Coming Event Key. Behind the key is a philosophy as powerful as any in human affairs—the threat of loss.

Remember what you learned earlier about capitalizing buyer fears? The avoid-less opportunity comes to you every day of the year. Dramatize the possibility of loss and the buyer is putty in your hands.

This closing technique, based upon one of the most vital desires of mankind, is effective because it has such a substantial foundation.

People are often unmoved by promise or satisfaction. But if people fear losing what they already have they'll almost invariably act promptly.

Chauncey Depew, raconteur and successful businessman, described this desire to avoid loss this way:

"If a man came to my house," he told a group of friends, "at three o'clock in the morning, awakened me, and told me that by going downstairs I could make $100, I'd kick him downstairs and go back to bed. So would every one of you."

He would pause, and then add:

"But if the same man woke me and told me by getting up, dressing, and going with him I could *avoid the loss* of $100, I'd say: 'Just wait till I get my pants on.' I'd go with him. So would anyone.

"The fear of loss is one of the strongest fears in life," Depew concluded.

SHOW NEED FOR ACTION

The Coming Event Key trades on this desire to avoid loss—no matter what it costs. You use it by pointing out that if the buyer fails to take advantage of what you're offering, he or she's going to suffer irremediable loss because of some impending event or action.

Note the subtle difference between this appeal and telling how much the customer will *profit* if he or she buys. The avoid-loss appeal is infinitely stronger and more moving. It practically never fails because it's rooted so deeply in human nature.

To use this technique, you bring up some impending event that requires action at the moment of closing. The event itself is of little consequence. Retail stores use it in advertising: "On May 15, prices will be advanced 10 percent." The message: buy now to avoid the loss.

This appeal works even when the loss is *implied*. Witness the gasoline station in New Jersey just outside the Holland Tunnel. As motorists approach the tunnel entrance leading to Manhattan, they see a large sign: *Last chance to buy gas in Jersey*. The station has done booming business for years. After all, if this is the last chance, better get it. (What the station doesn't say, of course is that when you get through the tunnel, you'll get your *first* chance to buy gasoline in New York.)

Another example: the con-man who ran the classified ad: *This is your last chance to send me a dollar*—followed by his address. Thousands sent in dollar bills.

"Last chance," they thought. "Better get in on it before we *lose.*"

The principle works equally well on the ethical selling firing-line. The saleswoman reminds you the business lot you want will be optioned at three o'clock. She suggests if you don't act quickly, you won't have a chance to get it at all. After three o'clock you'll suffer loss.

You do not want to suffer loss, so you decide to buy now, even though you might have wanted to think it over longer. If what the saleswoman told you about the impending event is true, there is nothing wrong with this technique. (Of course, unscrupulous salespeople lie about impending events and it may work for a short time. But once buyers get onto a four-flusher, as they do, it doesn't work any more.)

The clothing salesman tells you the suit you're undecided about is the only one of its kind left. Furthermore, another customer, who looked at it yesterday, will be in again at noon.

"But of course you're here now," he tells you, "and if you decide, I'll have to tell Doctor Elliot he's too late." You buy. The Coming Event moved you along.

The life insurance salesperson comes in the day before your age changes: you'll be out $10 per $1000 if you wait until tomorrow. That's $10 per $1000 lost *overnight!* You never want to take a loss like that if you can help it. You may not have been quite ready for more insurance. But the prospect of losing if you don't buy is more than you can stand. You buy to avoid the loss.

The coming event can be a condition. The prospect wants to postpone decision. You tell him of the small quantity you have left of a certain item. Retail stores use this in limited quantity sales. One mail-order enterprise sold 100,000 sets of books by pointing out that only a few more sets were available.

The possibility of being left out, of losing something, is too much for the average prospect and he or she buys when this technique is properly used.

OVERCOMING DELAY

Although *Do It Now* is the great American maxim, many buyers—as every salesperson knows—are terribly inclined to wait until *mañana*: "I'll think it over and perhaps buy later." The Coming Event helps you overcome procrastination, the chief enemy of salesfolk everywhere, and close the buyer who's inclined to postpone.

Your prospect says he's not quite ready. He asks you to see him next week or call him Wednesday.

"I'll be glad to do that, Mr. Watterson," you tell him, "but I am afraid that Wednesday, or next week, will be too late."

"Why?"

"Because—" and then you tell him the event or condition, a rise in price, or inability to get the merchandise you're talking about.

If this coming event is a certainty, you are not risking anything. If he really wants your product, you're only pushing him to buy now rather than later. If the coming event is not a certainty, but merely a probability, you can still make a good case for it.

"Now, I won't take an oath that the price of this paper will advance from 20 to 40 percent in the next 30 days," a paper salesman told me. "I don't know. But this I do know. If the past is any indication, I may be erring on the conservative side to predict price increases of a mere 40 percent. Let me show you what the market did 20 years ago, when conditions were almost identical with conditions today."

Using actual figures of two decades ago, he convinced me that if I did not buy now, that coming event (expected and not guaranteed) would cause me loss. Of course, I bought. My fear of losing if I did not buy was greater than my unwillingness to buy until I had thought the matter over.

THE DRAMATIC GESTURE

You can *create* a Coming Event. Richard Considine is a master in closing with the dramatic gesture.

Dick Considine is president of Lincoln Logs Ltd., Chestertown, NY. He was the company's first salesman and he remains the driving force behind the company's sales success. One day at 5 p.m., right after he founded the innovative housing firm, the telephone rang. George Jones, from Rochester, wanted to inquire about a log home. Dick described the advantages and how easy it is to build on a do-it-yourself basis. Jones was interested but was not decisive. After all, a $9000-$15,000 home is a big-ticket decision.

Dick wheeled in the *created* coming event.

"Mr. Jones," he said, mentally canceling his evening's plans, "I'm three hours away from you. I'm going out to get in my car and drive to Rochester. I'll be there before 8 p.m. tonight. I'm sure we can work out this log home for you."

By 9 p.m. Dick Considine had a $1000 check as a binding deposit. The dramatic gesture had closed the sale.

"Anytime I get buying signals from a prospect, I drop what I'm doing and help them make a decision," Dick Considine says. "Any salesperson who doesn't put closing ahead of *everything* isn't a real closer."

Dick's selling philosophy has rocketed Lincoln Logs to industry leadership.

"FOUR MEN HERE TOMORROW"

Tom Tierney, who sells a business consulting service to top management, draws on a similar technique. After describing his service and his top people, Tom moves in for the close.

"Mr. Smythe, you've heard us outline what we plan to do in solving your problems. This will require us to sit down with your top people and get quite a bit of data as our first step in doing the job. My plan is to have four men here tomorrow."

Immediately, the prospect became involved in hosting the four visitors, who they should see, when this should be scheduled, etc. Or he may say the day after tomorrow is a better day.

Obviously, the sale is closed—by a coming event.

NERVOUS BREAKDOWN AS EVENT

Albert D. Lasker, in his day the nation's best and richest advertising man, worked himself into a nervous breakdown.

While in the hospital, he got word that a certain prospect meeting was set. It was the critical closing opportunity.

Lasker fought off nurses and doctors, jumped into his clothes, and arrived at the meeting where the corporate brass were talking in millions.

"Gentlemen, I came here to get your account for my firm," he said. "I have no business being here. I am in the hospital having a nervous breakdown. Now if you will sign these contracts, I will return to the hospital and finish the job of getting well."

Lasker was master of the controlled coming event—even his own breakdown!

Many times in your own selling you'll find you can use The Coming Event Key as the strongest possible closing lever. Naturally, if you go around predicting impending events that cannot possibly happen, you destroy confidence. Use it honestly and with discretion. Stick to facts. Dig out new facts to make it work, if need be.

The Coming Event Key frequently ushers in *another* Coming Event—the closing of your sale.

THE THIRD PARTY ENDORSEMENT KEY

15

WHEN YOU USE the Third Party Endorsement Key in closing sales, you recruit someone else—usually an expert or a respected colleague of the customer—to tell your story for you. As a salesperson, you're assumed to be less than objective about your product. The third party has no axe to grind and, therefore, has high credibility.

Morris I. Pickus, Los Angeles selling genius, calls the endorser the Friendly Third Party. Pickus will not make a sales call alone. He always takes the FTP along.

During the sale, Pickus will cite his FTP, knowing that the prospect, being imitative as all human beings are, is interpreting success of the third party as his own.

"If he can do it, I can do it," the prospect is thinking.

Frank H. Davis, a master salesman, is talking to an important prospect. The sale has reached the point where an experimental close is in order. Davis recognizes the buying signal, so he launches an effective narrative close.

At the moment of closing, he tells his customer a story. The customer listens. He is enthralled. He leans forward, so as not to miss a word. He imagines himself in place of the characters in the story. Their situations he likens to his own, for that is human nature. He sees point by point the parallel between what they lacked and what he now lacks.

Immediately he senses the wisdom of the solution they found, which is buying what Frank Davis is selling. When Davis deftly places the order blank in front of him, the customer signs. He is glad to. He has been completely sold.

Frank Davis is brilliant in using the Friendly Third Party Key in closing. His work is a beautiful example of the power in this interesting technique.

TELL A RELATED STORY

Often the Friendly Third Party Key consists of telling a business story. The purpose of this story is not entertainment (it may be entertaining as a bonus). Your purpose is to make the customer see himself in the light of another experience. It works. Each one of us imitates. We follow, with childlike faith, if the proper examples are held in front of us.

Consider yourself in a buying mode (as we all are frequently). When a salesperson relates the experience of someone in business whom we respect or admire, you immediately say: "If he could do it in such a manner, I can do it in the same way."

Whenever we are given half a chance, we imitate. The shrewd closer of sales gives customers a chance to employ this imitative tendency.

MOVIE STORIES

Breakstone Tally was a great salesman, perhaps the greatest. But he could have become a novelist or screenwriter. He was an enormously effective teller of stories. His stories gripped you, put you into the picture, made you want to act. His stories enabled him to control thousands of prospects.

"Tell your prospects movie stories," Tally advised, "to close more sales."

Movie stories involve someone whose situation resembles the prospect's. You're selling merchandise to retail stores. You want the prospect to buy. He is reluctant. Time for a movie story.

When you first called on a certain store (which you know your prospect knows) the certain store told you the same thing—no demand for your goods. But the store decided to try the products anyway.

And with what results! You cite actual figures. You show vast profits. You point out new customers. And your prospect drools.

THE CONNER AND TEDMON STORY

Stone Wheaton tells movie stories better than most. Listen as he works toward the close with retailer John P. Atter:

"Do you know Conner and Tedmon of Nashville?"

Very well, John Atter says.

"What do you think of them as businessmen?"

Atter says they've built a tremendous business in Nashville in face of great competition.

That's Wheaton's go-signal. He launches into his story of what Conner and Tedmon have done in Nashville with the products he's suggesting to Atter. He tells the Conner and Tedmon story in a running narrative. Everybody likes an interesting story.

When he first called upon Conner and Tedmon, Wheaton relates, he found such and such a condition prevailed. (It "happens" to be almost exactly the same business condition John Atter faces.) Mr. Conner wasn't exactly sure whether Wheaton's products would correct the condition and give him what he needed in profit. (Neither is Atter sure at this particular moment.)

As an experiment—but only as an experiment—Mr. Conner decided to put in Wheaton's line. (That gives John Atter courage: maybe he also could try it. Here's a respected precedent to follow.)

"But now Conner and Tedmon are thanking their lucky stars they experimented," Wheaton says. "Sales increased 30 percent in a year's time. Their turnover has speeded up. Profit is better than ever. They have attracted a new type of customer."

Thus does Stone Wheaton talk, confirming his statements, of course, with evidence.

He's, in effect, saying: "Don't take my word for it. Follow someone else who's already done the experimenting for you."

Meanwhile, John Atter is telling himself that if Conner and Tedmon can make such a record with the line, he can do as well, maybe better. Further, Conner and Tedmon's acceptance of the product line is a recommendation for him to accept it— evidence to overcome his own wavering and cause him to buy.

In every case, when you use the Third Party Endorsement, the prospect unconsciously, if not consciously, compares his business to the character in the narrative. Success of the central figure in the story is *his* success—if he does what you suggest (which is to buy). The prospect thus sells himself. You don't need difficult, intricate, or high-pressure closing methods.

Stone Wheaton closed the sale. The Third Party did it.

The Friendly Third Party assumes various forms. Telling stories is perhaps the most common. The testimonial letter is another. A customer or client list is a third.

We're all fascinated by the opinion of others. Obviously, we believe another user quicker than we believe the seller.

TESTIMONIALS

Very early in business history, sellers found that testimonials—the opinions of users—proved powerful in bringing about conviction.

Salespeople started using testimonials by word of mouth, quoting a user. But testimonial letters on the user's letterhead or in his own words are even more effective.

Some salespeople carry around a book of photocopied testimonial letters. The more you have, the better. A large volume of testimonial letters overpowers buyer resistance.

Any letter from a *person* your prospect knows—or knows about—is worth twice as much. Next best is a *company* the prospect knows or knows about.

A successful mail-order merchant discovered sales letters including a testimonial from a satisfied user pulled a healthy number of orders. If the testimonial came from a townsman of the reader, the results were markedly more effective.

The cue for you: get letters from buyers your prospect knows, either in person or by reputation.

An effective use of testimonial letters by a Chicago industrial sales manager is called The Avalanche. Instead of testimonial letters bound in a sales kit, he tells his reps to carry loose letters.

At closing time, the salesrep brings out one testimonial letter, hands it to the prospect, lets him glance at it, hands him another as soon as he puts it down, hands him a third. Soon the prospect's desk is literally covered with testimonial letters.

The more letters, the better. No prospect can see his desk covered with comments by satisfied users and not be sold on the product.

THE CUSTOMER LIST

This is an effective form of Third Party. Salespeople should use it more than they do. Compile a list of prominent customers. The list builds confidence and actually helps close the sale. Salesfolk who sell book or magazine subscriptions, two rather difficult sells, almost always use a customer list in closing.

One expert magazine salesman carried a long list of many pages. The customers' names were in their own handwriting, which made them more effective. He put this list on my desk.

"We are mighty proud of our customers, you know," he said to me.

"You know Judge Hollister of the Supreme Court, don't you?"

"Oh, yes."

"There is his name. I expect you know Andrew Read, president of the Nationwide Manufacturing Company."

He chatted interestingly about the names and then said: "Here are the types of people who have taken advantage of this offer. People like..." and he read some more prominent names. "You know what people of that caliber are, what their judgment is. I want to put your name down alongside that of Judge Hollister and Mayor Preston."

Without going into any other kind of sales argument, he closed the majority of his prospects. Only he really didn't close them. They closed themselves.

The imitative faculty is so strong in each of us that *it* closes sales. All you do is steer it in the right channels—the Third Party Endorsement.

STORYTELLING POWER

One of the greatest sales managers the world has ever known, a man with a really scientific mind, told me he'd discovered the one bright and shining quality that guarantees success in selling.

"All my life I've been looking for just such information," I told him. "What's your discovery?"

"Why, he must be a good storyteller," said my friend. "That doesn't mean remembering and relating risqué stories. The salesperson must be able to *interest* people."

We know some personalities are interesting. Others are not. We'd much prefer to be classified among interesting personalities. A colorless person can hardly become an ace salesman or saleswoman. An interesting personality nearly always has the ability to tell interesting things. As the great author Anatole France said: "For pleasure and profit, there is nothing like stories."

Storytelling constitutes one of the really great secrets of closing sales through the Third Party Endorsement.

USE MEMORABLE CHARACTERS

Frank Davis—there was a great salesman for you! He was strong in every department of salesmanship. In ten years he rose from Missouri hillside farmer to vice-president of one of the world's largest life insurance companies. He did it through sheer selling ability—through sheer *closing* ability, actually.

At least half of Davis' greatness rested upon his ability to use the storytelling close. He told closing stories to the high, to the low, to the old, to the young. His methods? So obvious it was astonishing customers didn't see through them! But they never did. They were enthralled. They never knew or forgot it was a selling technique.

Davis had favorite stories he told in closing sales about experiences of men and women with insurance. He told these stories logically, naturally, with ease, charm, and high interest. He told them so well that listeners saw themselves reaping the benefits. They couldn't help buying.

Frank Davis believed heartily in stories. He went to great lengths to make every single detail correct. He studied words. He studied the characters to make sure they had memorable names. His two main characters were Homer McGillicuddy and Helen Barley. Why these names?

"Homer McGillicuddy and Helen Barley are memorable," said this great salesman. "They get into your bloodstream. No one hearing those names can ever forget them."

He was right. I've never forgotten those names nor the stories about them. What a master Frank Davis was!

Once Davis was talking with Conway Kremer, a crusty executive and the hardest of prospects to sell. Kremer didn't like Davis, didn't like anyone or anything. He was insolent, insulting, destestable.

The sale didn't appear to be progressing very well. Kremer, through his antagonism, had Davis stymied at every turn.

"An accident occurred in Chicago last week that made me think of you, Mr. Kremer," said Davis, and a story close was on its way.

Interested at once because he was the central figure, Kremer said: "Is that so?"

"I stopped in at the Sherman House and walked up to the cigar stand and said: 'Give me a Corona.' I didn't pay any attention to the woman behind the counter until I heard her say: 'Frank!' I looked. I said: 'Why, Helen!' It took me so by surprise. 'Helen, what are you doing here?' I finally asked."

'Why Frank, haven't you heard?'

"Heard...heard what?"

'About George?'

"No. Don't tell me he's...."

She began to cry. 'Yes,' she said, 'George is gone. He passed away six weeks ago.'

"No!"

'He died very suddenly. One night he came home, the picture of health. Two days later he was dead.'

"She sobbed harder. It seemed indelicate to ask her if he had left her comfortably fixed. But presently she told me all about it.

"George hadn't believed in life insurance," Davis continued with his story. "He always told me 'Frank, don't kid me. I can invest my own money better than any insurance company can.' He was absolutely sincere. He believed it. But his investments hadn't turned out. And his wife, Helen Barley, was back behind the counter selling cigars.

"When I told you, Mr. Kremer, that it reminded me of you, what I meant was this: George Barley looked a great deal like you. You always reminded me of him. Of course, what happened to him couldn't possibly happen to you. But no one could have read the sorrow and reproach in that poor widow's eyes without being moved by the deep responsibility each of us has to our families."

Conway Kremer, that hard-boiled, self-satisfied executive, who five minutes before was browbeating Davis, said: "I've reconsidered. How soon can you have me examined for insurance?"

He saw himself in George Barley's position. He saw his own wife in Helen Barley's position. He didn't want that. So he bought the insurance.

Frank Davis used this powerful technique in closing sales. Use it in closing yours. On hearing a story, your prospect will immediately identify himself with characters. In the process of identifying, the buyer sells himself on what you want him to do.

SOFTENING HARD CASES

Evangeline Booth of the Salvation Army used similar techniques in converting hardened criminals. She had a closing job, too. She tried to reason with these men, and got nowhere. She tried to appeal to their sense of pride. They had none. But by hitching on to an idea that came from within them, she made the most unregenerate criminals weaken and sob.

She started with memories of the convict's childhood. She asked him questions about his mother. The hard case could resist anything from the outside, but against ideas from within himself, he was powerless.

AVOID THIN ICE

In telling your stories, don't make heroes out of characters the buyer has no confidence in or respect for. Remember the Conner and Tedmon story? First the salesperson asked if his prospect *knew* them. The prospect said he admired Conner and Tedmon. Only then did the salesperson tell his story. If the prospect said he didn't think much of these two men, the salesperson would have said: "I believe I can understand your feeling, Mr. Haber. But I think you'll agree that they're pretty good retailers, won't you?"

With a *yes* answer, he could use the example or quickly try another name instead.

Observe this precaution before plunging into the narrative. When your stories have conviction, they are a most useful selling tool. Stories close sales easily, naturally, pleasantly—and definitely.

INTEREST IS ABSOLUTELY VITAL

Bergen Evans, famed Northwestern English professor and TV personality, was once asked in rather academic language how his teaching method differed from the norm. Evans wrote simply:

"I have tried to be *interesting!*"

That's a small, but vital, distinction. A distinction that made him a personality on three TV shows and much in demand on the lecture circuit.

Try to be interesting! It's a tremendous trifle. You must tell your stories so well the distracted prospect will gladly listen. Telling stories well is an art. Some salespeople can tell any kind of story with spontaneity and interest. Others belabor their points and bore you to tears. Stories that labor, drag, miss the point, or tire are not going to assist you very much in getting business.

What you must do, therefore, is learn how to tell stories well. The answer lies in one word—*practice*. Spend hours, if need be, perfecting them. Rehearse just as carefully as an actor rehearses his lines. Tape yourself. If you don't like what you hear, take a public speaking course.

Back before TV, staff radio announcers read commercials. When TV emerged, announcers were soon replaced in commercials by actors. Today a large coterie of actors does nothing but TV commercials—along with a host of famous performers who do commercials in addition to their screen and stage work.

Says Peter Walker, a New York actor known for his Volkswagen and Tegrin commercials:

"I work just as hard or harder on my selling roles as on a stage part. The point is to make the character believable and interesting. Once I've done that, the product—assuming it has basic merit—will come across fine."

There is a strong relationship between acting and selling. The actor has to create a favorable impression. So does the salesperson. The actor has to convince. So does the salesperson. The best salespeople look upon their work just as an actor looks upon his. They go through the same routine in perfecting—rehearsal and more rehearsal.

A champion salesman's wife described her husband's rehearsal:

"He'll walk for hours in front of the mirror," she said, "going through his act. He smiles, not at all self-consciously, becomes serious, uses gestures, taps his palm, sits down, arises. He demonstrates for the mirror in the bedroom."

That careful preparation has paid handsome dividends. When he tells his stories, people are glad to listen.

Nearly all great leaders have paid more attention to perfection in their presentations than the average person ever dreams is possible.

THE EMPEROR'S CLOSE

Napoleon, as self-assured a person as ever lived, realized the necessity for special training in making important pronouncements to his people. Before he was crowned emperor of France, he hired the best actor available. They spent hours rehearsing what he would say and do on his great day. He went through every gesture, perfected every word. When he got up in front of the multitude and told his story, it stuck.

So will your narrative closes, if you pay the attention to perfecting them that Napoleon paid.

One Detroit sales manager believes firmly in this. He puts young salespeople through a dramatic course after they demonstrate initial ability. This costs his firm money. Occasionally management gets on his back about costs. But he always demonstrates that each dollar spent on dramatics training is worth $100 in profit.

"The average person is inarticulate in facial expression," he says. "He needs training. The sales trainee learns easily enough how to control words. But unless he or she has some professional trianing, they'll never learn how to control face and expressions. You must not register disappointment, anger, disgust, or any state-of-mind so effective in driving orders away.

"I want my salespeople to be actors so they can control their facial expressions, and not reveal what they're really thinking."

Learn to communicate and not communicate what you're thinking—and when to do each. Many ace closers are also good poker players. It's *not* a coincidence. A winning poker player is also an accomplished actor—fully adept at telling stories that sell by Third-Party power.

THE SOMETHING FOR
NOTHING KEY

16

WE SPEND our lives trying to find something for nothing. We never succeed—really. There's no free lunch. But does that keep us from trying again and again? Not at all.

The desire to get something free is the basis for a powerful closing key—Something for Nothing.

Something for Nothing works because human nature loves a bargain. This is universal. A man once got a call about an unusual bargain in elephant sandwiches. An entire carload was suddenly available. Quality was A-1—the best elephant sandwiches on earth.

"But I'm a vegetarian," the man told the caller. "I eat no meat. Even if I did, I don't believe in killing off endangered species. On top of that. I'm on a liquid diet. Doctor's orders. There's no way you could possibly sell me any elephant sandwiches."

The caller remained calm.

"I forgot to tell you," he said. "These elephant sandwiches are only 25 cents apiece."

The buyer changed his tune.

"Now you're talking *my language*," he said.

A fantastic bargain. Almost Something for Nothing. It's a powerful appeal.

Of course, the prospect *knows* he gets what he pays for and not a bit more. But he keeps on hoping to get Something for Nothing. This means you must keep this closing key brightly shined and in strong working order.

Something for Nothing is workable because it overcomes one of your most powerful adversaries—procrastination.

The saleswoman promises the prospect something extra—it can be something of no consequence whatsoever—and the prospect, hard-headed and crafty otherwise, falls like an axed steer and buys.

Many times, you find the customer willing enough to listen, easy enough to interest. She believes what you say. She wants your product, there is no doubt about that. But when it comes to saying the final word, to taking the final step, she balks. Puts you off. The sale bogs down. And there you are. Nothing you said or did brought the transaction to such a state of procrastination. This democratic force, as inexorable as the law of gravity, is working against you.

Right now you are going to discover a closing technique that recognizes procrastination and enables you to close in spite of it.

Something for Nothing, as the name implies, offers the buyer a special inducement if he will buy now. The technique plays upon a sense of loss if the customer fails to act now.

HOLD FREEBIE IN RESERVE

Something for Nothing is best used as a final inducer. Hold it in reserve until the end. This sales inducer is based on a fundamental human appeal—the desire to get something special not generally available, something exclusive. This technique takes advantage of the weakness inherent in all of us. It offers something valuable or something trivial, something real or something fancied, and shows us that we will lose if we don't take advantage of it. So we buy to avoid the possibility of loss.

A woman went into a restaurant and asked the price for a bacon-and-egg sandwich.

"Two dollars and forty cents," the waiter said.

"How many eggs?"

"One egg."

"How many slices of bacon?"

"Two."

She thought a while, shook her head, and started to leave. Before she reached the door the waiter yelled: "But, Madam, the bread is absolutely free."

She bought the sandwich. She couldn't resist the free bread.

Your success in using the Something for Nothing Key in closing sales depends on *how* and *when* you use it. Sometimes the inducement is the only strategy that will get you the order. Sometimes you can close without it. Wise salespeople, therefore, hold Something for Nothing as a last resort. Use it only if everything else fails.

MOBILITY IN CLOSING

Pierre Vendome, a French Canadian mobile home dealer, was an adroit SFN user. He always added the cost of a hitch ($55 retail) to each mobile home model before he quoted the price. When the customer wavered or talked about visiting other dealers, Vendome would say:

"Wait! I will do *eenythin'* to get you to buy today. I'll *geef* you this hitch which costs $55. *Eenythin'* to get you to buy today."

The couple, seeing their chance to get a free hitch, often bought. Vendome threw in the hitch only at the last minute. If he didn't need it, he didn't use it. He just made $55 more on the sale. Something for Nothing. It works.

The idea is not to shoot all your arrows immediately. Hold one in reserve, the inducement you're prepared to offer *if* it becomes necessary. Try to close the customer with one of the other secret or special keys first. But suppose the buyer remains adamant. You need something special. Trot out Something for Nothing.

When you bring out your inducer, you are offering the buyer an entirely new and more favorable proposition. The inducer immediately freshens your appeal. It brings you more interest. When you feel a sale slipping, when all efforts to close verge on failure, bring out the inducer. Explain it. Make the buyer feel the sense of loss if he or she doesn't take advantage of it. It will close sales.

GREAT VALUE NOT NEEDED

Auntie Mame said: "Life's a bowl of cherries and most poor bastards are starving to death." She could have added: "Yes, and on the prime lookout for something free of charge." Or, at least, the *illusion* of free.

The inducer can be almost anything. A piece of trivia, not worth more than a few cents, often pushes sales worth several thousands of dollars over the line.

Fred C. Kelly learned this truth selling houses. A fancier of collies, Kelly usually took a puppy along when showing a house. One day, Carson and Esmeralda Brown were considering a $150,000 home. They liked the house and the view. But the price—aye, there was the rub. The Browns hadn't intended to pay $150,000. Besides, there were certain things they didn't entirely like—the arrangement of rooms, closet space, etc.

The sale was on the rocks. Kelly had given up all hope. Then the wife looked at the pup, and asked if he went with the house. Kelly replied:

"He certainly does. What home would be complete without a dog?"

Mrs. Brown said they'd better buy. Mr. Brown agreed. The deal was closed. The special inducement in a $150,000 sale was a collie pup!

This non-expensive inducer might have been more influential than a more valuable advantage. Kelly had experimented with different inducers: cherry trees and lawn swings enabled him to make sales against competitors who had the edge in price and value. The inducers, worth little in actual money, far outweighed real advantages. We all want something for nothing. But nothing worked as well as a warm, tail-wagging puppy.

Back in vaudeville days, comedian Fred Allen recalled playing a town so far back in the woods the assistant manager of the hotel was a bear! Animals provide that extra benefit!

Think about the way clever promoters presented vaudeville acts—starting with the headliners. But they always held one back. At the bottom of the poster, in larger type, the theatergoer read: *Extra! Added! John Simplon and His Talking Dogs!* A Something for Nothing.

If you have difficulty in closing a sale, introduce an inducement. Almost anything special will do—some insignificant price advantage, perhaps something of a personal nature. It really doesn't matter much what the inducement is, as long as it appeals to the prospect.

YOUR NAME IN GOLD

Perry Waters was having difficulty selling a $15 book—until he started using Something for Nothing. He raised the price to $17.95 and offered to put the buyer's name on the cover in gold—*free* to each purchaser. Sales went up 200 percent! Offer something that seems like a great benefit—free.

The floor salesman in the music department was having difficulty in closing an obdurate prospect. He tried several closing techniques. Nothing happened. He decided to use inducement.

"I'l tell you what I'll do, Mr. Matson," the salesman said. "I'll give you this record brush as a free gift, if you will place your order today. It's a token of our appreciation for getting your order this week."

Don't be afraid to *give* in order to *get*. Remember the words of Winston Churchill:

"We make a living by what we *get*. We make a life by what we *give*."

BIGGER PIECE OF PIE

Claude Hopkins, one of the greatest mass salesmen America has ever produced, worked in Chicago for a meat packer. A special problem was dumped in his lap: selling expensive shortening to commercial bakers. The packer's six salespeople in Boston had sold practically no shortening in a month.

The packing house owner called Hopkins in and said:

"Here is a letter from Boston. I agree with it entirely. They are not making sales and cannot make sales at the price you have fixed on our product."

"They are wrong," Hopkins said. "Real salesmanship isn't concerned about price."

The boss said: "Can you sell to the bakers in Boston?"

"I believe I could."

"Can you go this afternoon?"

"Yes."

When Hopkins arrived in Beantown, he asked the local manager to name the hardest prospect of all. He got the name: Ebenezer Fox, owner of the Fox Pie Company. Fox wasn't particularly eager to see Hopkins.

"I came from Chicago to consult you about a card," Hopkins said, placing a card about five feet away. He explained further, "That card is intended to picture the ideal pie. It cost us a great deal of money. The artist charged us $500 for the drawing."

After much discussion, Fox declared the card pictured pie at its best, and that if he could make pies like that, Fox would have the largest market share in Boston.

"How many Boston stores are selling Fox pies?" asked Hopkins.

"About 1,000."

"Mr. Fox," Hopkins said, "I'll give you a card like that to go in every store. I will give you 250 of those cards with every carload of shortening you order now, as a special offer."

The prospect bought four carloads of shortening on the spot. Then Hopkins went to Providence, to New Haven, to Hartford, to Springfield, and he sold more orders than the six salespeople had sold in six weeks.

The local manager was scornful.

"You haven't been selling shortening," he said. "You have been selling a pie card. I'd like to see what you can do when you can't offer that. Do you think you could sell if you didn't have that card to offer?"

"Of course. Who would you want me to try?"

The manager named a large firm, which Hopkins called on the telephone, only to discover that the prospect—loaded up with shortening—was not interested in buying more. But a salesman like Hopkins does not permit a little thing like that to deter him. He suggested a special inducement:

"I want to suggest a way to advertise your pies all the way from here to Chicago. If you order two carloads, I will place a sign on both sides of the cars. That sign will announce that your pies are made with our product. Not on one side of the car, but on both sides, so everyone for 900 miles, on both sides of the tracks, will know you."

He sold two carloads to an overloaded customer. He knew how to use Something for Nothing.

Practically all the great business leaders—and that means great salespeople, because business is selling—are astute users of Something for Nothing.

MEN'S ROOM DIPLOMACY

If you followed the business methods of the late Howard Hughes—and most everyone did—then you know of his dedication to doing business in the men's room of public buildings. Hugh Edwards, president of The Research Guild, Atlanta, believes the men's room is also an excellent place to close with a psychic Something for Nothing.

Edwards had gone to Minneapolis to sell his research services to General Mills. But he was having a hard time getting to see Jerry Stoneseifer, the decision-maker. He had just about given up—after talking with several other receptive but non-decision-making people—when he spotted Stoneseifer on route to the men's room.

"Why not?" Edwards said and followed.

At adjacent stands inside, Edwards struck up a conversation and explained his business.

"We've been having a lot of trouble with our existing suppliers, getting them to understand the General Mills way," Stoneseifer said.

Edwards said he could understand that problem.

"Many suppliers are set in their ways," he said. "And it's hard to change them. But I guess it all depends on how you get started. Now us, we believe in helping you *train* your own suppliers—right from the start—in doing things your way. Remember what Dr. Samuel Johnson said: 'Much can be made of a Scotsman—if he is caught young.' With us, you can train your own research group *just as if we were located in the last office on the left*. Of course, the important difference is we're *not*. We bring you outside expertise and outside objectivity. It's a Something-for-Nothing value you get in working with us."

Well, Stoneseifer said, maybe you've got something there. Edwards went home with an assignment that led to many more. Shortly, he was doing close to $100,000 worth of business a year from General Mills.

"The idea of training his own suppliers *his* way did it," Edwards said. "He felt he was getting Something for Nothing. But somehow it wouldn't have worked in his office. I highly recommend the men's room for certain kinds of selling."

Everyone wants a little something more as the motorist found when he asked the Maine character:

"Have you lived here all your life?"

Said the Down-Easter, carefully whittling a piece of wood: "Not yet."

GUM KING USED SFN

The late William Wrigley, Jr., was eminently successful because he was continually sending his dealers special inducements to get them to buy more. One time Wrigley sent out a card listing a number of premiums dealers could earn by buying more gum.

Another time he would offer a bonus for orders of a minimum size. It was always something attractive, something special, something in the way of an inducement to buy.

Wrigley was using on a large scale the same technique you can use in your individual face-to-face contacts—Something for Nothing to close sales.

COUNSEL FOR FREE

Al Wall gives his customers Something for Nothing—free counsel. A Hollywood casting director would probably never cast Al Wall as a sales manager. (Movies, like the law, tend to lag considerably behind reality.) Al Wall is the modern, quiet salesperson who's come a long way from the old stereotype. He's racked up a successful record selling decorative home accessories—so much so he's now national sales manager of The MaLeck Group, a leading company in that field.

Al's Something for Nothing strategy is consulting. He meets regularly with group buyers for department store chains—not to sell—but to talk about their problems.

"Funny you never try to sell us your products," a buyer said to Al one day.

"No, I don't," Al said. "I'm here to find out about your problems and to relay solutions I've encountered among other retailers. Now some of those solutions probably include MaLeck products—and if so, I'll tell you. I'm not selling products. I'm offering solutions to business problems."

This approach, Al says, is the long-term way to sell. Give solutions to problems and you're always welcome. Sell products and you're only as good as your last sale.

Al Wall calls it reverse selling. His customers feel they're getting an added service for free. No wonder Al's company sales rose 20 percent last year.

THE GREENING INDUCEMENT

Terry and Sue Muth sell Lincoln Log homes in Haywarden, Iowa. They are also experts in landscaping and plants—that's their second business.

Sue Muth, who studied horticulture, decided to use greening as a Something for Nothing Key in closing home sales.

"Buy this log home and we'll give you $600 worth of landscaping free," the Muths tell customers.

It works. A recent customer signed up saying: "What a relief! I was wondering what to do about the grass and trees. What a nice addition."

Sometimes what would cost your customer $600 can be bought wholesale for $300—well worth it to nail down a big-ticket sale.

The inducement need not be tangible. It can be purely a mental picture. If you can show the buyer he will lose prestige by *not* buying now, that is an inducement. If you can show the buyer her name will go on an honor roll if she buys now, that is a sufficient inducement.

Or you can turn it around: "You are paying for this whether you are enjoying its advantages or not."

The Something for Nothing Key comes in mighty handy. You can often use it when everything else has failed. It tackles and whips the ever-present problem of procrastination—your worst enemy in selling. It appeals to that universal hope in everyone— "What's for free?"

THE ASK AND GET KEY

17

THE DISTINGUISHED BOARD was meeting to consider James Hyatt's proposal. It required an investment of $100,000.

There were conflicts. One member wanted it. Another said no. One said wait. And so it went on for half an hour, until Hyatt played his trump card—Ask and Get—one of the most powerful of all keys.

Curtain up.

"Gentlemen, you have all had your say. We have listened to much articulate talk. Now it's time for action. I want your order for this service and I want it now. Will you sign my order?"

Board: "Yes."

It was as simple as that—he merely asked for an order and he got an order.

Earlier you met a salesman named Blayney. His closing technique was based entirely on Ask and Get. He never used any other closing key. His methods were simple and often crude. These are verbatim closes he used:

"Jake, have you an order for me today?"

"Joe, are you going to buy from me today?"

"Mike, how about half a carload of bacon this morning?"

"Bill, here is a special we just brought out. I think you need 200 pounds as a starter."

To a man—Jake, and Joe, and Mike, and Bill, and Pete—went right along and bought what Blayney asked them to buy.

Yet there are some selling experts who say no salesperson should ever ask a prospect to buy. They say this makes you a beggar. Nonsense!

ASK A FAVOR TO WIN A FRIEND

Under certain conditions, asking for business is a very high type of salesmanship, if asked in the right way, and at the right time.

Opponents of this technique believe no salesperson should ever go to a prospect and ask a favor. But students of practical psychology know when you ask a favor, you really *do* a favor larger than the one you ask. When you ask a slight favor, you enhance his or her self-importance. They do the favor for you but actually they're favoring themselves. Therefore, when you ask a person to buy, you do not weaken your case. Quite often you strengthen it.

In fact, many sales managers believe asking for the order may be one of the best techniques. Some go further and say the only closing technique you need is asking for an order on every call. But that isn't altogether true.

ASK EARLY .

An interesting use of this method comes from Oxford Pendleton, a successful sales executive in Los Angeles.

"My plan is to ask the customer for the order at the earliest possible moment," Pendleton explains. "If he says 'Yes,' I'm in luck. If he says 'No,' he uses 50 words to explain, and I get a tip as to what's running through his mind. Having found out what he's thinking about, I continue my story until I can again ask for the order. The prospect either says 'Yes' or has to think up another 50 words.

"This goes on and on until I sell the item or throw in the towel. At least I can mentally say: 'That customer really had a chance to buy.' Most closing problems in selling are due to salespeople without guts enough to force an answer. Even the Bible says: 'Ask and it shall be given to you.' You can't beat that for authority!"

When you completely absorb this book, you'll have at your disposal a number of effective tested powerful closing techniques. Each is an ideal close in its own way. You can choose one for almost all conditions that arise in your day's selling. But there are times in selling when the best closing technique is simply asking the buyer frankly and openly for his or her business—the closing key in this chapter.

BUILDING FOUNDATION

A recent survey revealed that in approximately 45 percent of all sales calls, the salesperson fails to ask for the order. Many salespeople, even some with years of experience, turn chicken when it comes to close. They talk on and on, or worse, lapse into silence, hoping the customer will take the initiative.

Obviously, Ask and Get only works after you've built the right foundation. These principles will help you use Ask and Get.

1. Start closing at once. Start developing the factual base for closing as soon as you step through the door. Many assume that their presentation is complete when it really isn't—they've failed to establish facts; often they've just given their opinion. Remember the buyer must be convinced that the product being offered is the best one for him. The sooner you have a factual base, the better.

2. Convince the prospect you can help him. Never set the prospect up as an adversary. Watch out for the customer's best interests. It's basic, but it pays off. The buyer must live with the product and justify the decision to others. Make him feel like a hero, and you'll have a much better chance of getting a positive response when you move into the close.

3. Don't talk the order away. Many salespeople keep right on losing sales because they keep right on talking after the close should have been made. When the presentation is complete, all questions answered, all the roadblocks moved down, there is only one place to go: close. Any further talking can only be harmful.

In one situation it may mean bringing up new thoughts and possibilities that could suggest alternative courses of action to the prospect. In another situation you may wind up boring the prospect.

Whatever the case, each post-closing minute consumed with non-closing chitchat is another minute the prospect will have to think up a reason for not buying.

4. Maximize sales potential. Have an idea beforehand how much business a particular customer can do. Gear your presentation, and close accordingly. What do other customers similar in size and location buy? How much business does the customer do in comparable, but noncompetitive products? How much merchandise should he have on display and in stock? Is he properly geared to promote and merchandise the line? What's his financial condition?

Learn as much about customers and prospects as you can. Show customers and prospects how to market their goods more successfully. You're on your way to a mutually profitable business relationship.

WHEN OTHER KEYS FAIL

Under most ordinary selling circumstances, using one of the other closing keys is better than Ask and Get. Most other keys are more positive, more effective, less open to rejection than asking the buyer to give you the order.

Occasionally you meet a buyer who, for one reason or another, is not impressed or moved by the other techniques (so effective with most buyers). This occasional customer may be:

1. A suspicious person with an inferiority complex. The buyer is unsure of himself in everything, and hence unable to make up his mind. If anything you do makes him suspect you

are trying to close the sale, he gets out of hand, and doesn't buy, but shuts up like a clam and becomes impossible.

2. She may have strong vanity and want to be the big number in everything. She is best appealed to by playing on that sense of vanity or importance.

3. He may be a negative personality. He's antagonistic. He resents being controlled, guided, or led. Tell him a product is square, and he'll say it's round. Tell him it's black, and he'll try to prove it's white. Ordinary techniques do not work with such people. But asking them for business in the right way often does.

Sometimes you must tell such folk (The Contraries) the opposite of what you want done. Phil Taggart, who sells a financial relations service to top management in Houston, cites his Uncle Harry to illustrate this opposite-pole personality.

"My Uncle Harry is a Contrary," Taggart says. "If his wife wants to get him out to dinner, she must call and say she'd like to fix dinner at home. 'Oh, no,' Harry always says. 'I want to eat out.'

"If she wants to visit relatives on the East Coast, she suggests to Harry they go West. 'Oh, no,' he replies, 'It's high time we went East.' The only way to get him to take any action is to suggest just the opposite."

The corollary in selling is to suggest to The Contrary he or she cannot afford to buy at this time or that perhaps this product isn't for him or her.

The chief benefit of the Ask and Get Key is that it makes difficult customers realize their self-importance. Each of us has this sense. In difficult customers, it's more highly developed. When you ask a difficult buyer for his business, you do not need to demean yourself or appear servile. Ask for business in the right way and you're a person who does the buyer a favor by asking for one!

We all enjoy doing favors more than we enjoy receiving them. Doing a favor, provided it doesn't cause too much expense or trouble, brings us far more good than it brings the receiver. It protects and buoys our ego.

Henry I. McGee, dynamic president of Dallas Airmotive, always told his executive staff:

"Never let me hear about you making any call to a customer or prospective customer without asking for the order—no matter what stimulated your original call."

Jerry Grossman, likable manager of Wurlitzer's New York store, said it differently:

"If you don't ask, you don't get."

Whatever your style, ask.

When you simply and forthrightly ask a buyer for business, it shows you appreciate her, that she's important to you, that you recognize her importance by asking her for business. You may actually be employing one of the highest forms of closing when you adroitly employ the Ask and Get Key.

WHY ELSE DO YOU WANT TO BUY?

Mehdi Fakharzadeh, a millionaire insurance salesman,* carries the Ask and Get Key further when he runs into a roadblock. Rather than asking for the order, he asks: "Why *else* do you want to buy?"

Once Mehdi worked for weeks to get a difficult client to sign up for a $250,000 policy. The backing-and-forthing was unusually long. Finally, the man agreed to take his medical examination. Even this took longer than usual. At last the answer came from the underwriting department: "Rejected. We consider this applicant uninsurable."

A severe disappointment to Mehdi? All that work for nothing? Mehdi didn't see it that way.

Always a believer in person-to-person meetings, Mehdi went to see the applicant. He explained the rejection in detail. He expressed his honest regret. Then he probed the man's motives.

"I know a lot of reasons why you want this policy," he said, "and they're good reasons. But isn't there something else you were trying to do?"

The client, an import-export executive, admitted it.

---

*From *Mehdi: Nothing Is Impossible,* already cited in Chapter 11.

"Yes," he said. "I wanted to provide for my daughter and son-in-law. Now I can't."

Here was the real need.

"There is another way to do it," Mehdi said. "Suppose I come up with a plan (he always talks about a plan, never about insurance) which provides tax savings in the event of your son-in-law's or daughter's death. I'm sure you'll agree this is desirable."

The man was interested.

Mehdi started the ball rolling again. He analyzed the estates of the son-in-law and daughter. Soon he came back with two policies totaling $550,000. The father signed the initial check and the policies have been in force ever since.

Mehdi more than doubled his commission over the original policy. He saw problem as opportunity. He asked "Why else?"

Ed Trabulsy, sales manager at Mehdi's Metropolitan District Sales Office in Manhattan, says this ability to turn problems into opportunity makes the rare superstar.

"Supersalesmen like Mehdi just don't think negatively," Trabulsy said. "Mehdi never broods over setbacks. He looks at every problem as an opportunity. He glories in problems because he's sure he can find the way out. He always does. Maybe we will not all be superstars, but everyone, no matter what his production, can do better if he remembers Mehdi's advice: nothing is impossible.

"He starts with native charm, and he capitalizes on it all the way. He's sincere, never tries to fool anyone. He motivates himself. He believes 'sufficient unto the day is the evil thereof'—he doesn't import problems from yesterday or anticipate problems for tomorrow. He treats today's challenges today," Trabulsy said.

"His product knowledge is astounding. He spends time on each objection and he solves it. I gave up supervision of 30 men in another office to work with Mehdi. He's the finest salesman the company has ever had."

The same principles are available to you. Take charge of yourself. Analyze each problem to find the opportunity potential. It's always there somewhere.

KEEP TRYING TO CLOSE

The *time* you ask for the order is important, too. First decide which of the other keys is the most natural and most adaptable to the specific selling situation. Then try to close. Don't be dismayed if you fail with one, two, or even half-a-dozen experimental closes. As long as you get the opportunity, continue to try to close.

If everything else fails, you still have Ask and Get. If you do that in the right way, you're likely to flatter and win the buyer's esteem. And into the bargain, you may well close because vanity is powerful and ego is a dominant factor. If buyer ego and vanity are sufficiently stimulated by you asking for business, you may well close then and there. If your prospect's a psychological problem type just discussed, you may decide to *start* with the Ask and Get Key before experimenting with the other techniques.

ALWAYS ASK

A New York sales executive sent out a bulletin to his salesforce: "Hereafter, no matter what the conversation with the customer has been or how the interview has terminated, the last thing you must do before taking leave (provided he or she has not already bought) is to ask for the order."

Basic? Sure. Had each salesperson been doing it? No. They tried it for a month and it increased sales 25 percent! Asking each prospect to buy brought in a one-fourth increase in business. This is not an isolated case.

General Electric increased over-the-counter sales of Mazda lamps the same way. After careful experimentation, a sales executive devised a simple closing technique. Retail salespeople selling these lamps were required to ask everyone who stopped to look at a sparkling lamp display to buy a carton of eight bulbs. That was all. Just ask them to buy. One in four bought. Sales went up 25 percent.

If you ask for the order, there are only two things the buyer can do: buy or refuse. Occasionally the buyer will refuse. There is no denying that. But even if it happens, the buyer develops greater respect for you because he or she perceives how important they really are to you.

Never fail to ask your customer for the order. It works.

POLISH AND SOCKS

Kinney Shoe Stores carried socks and shoe polish for some time displayed behined the register. Some customers motivated themselves by asking for socks or polish as they checked out their shoe purchases.

Then one day an enterprising regional manager (he was new, and didn't know all the reasons why things won't work) said:

"From now on, we're going to *ASK* each customer to buy socks and polish. Just ask. Nothing more."

Each retail salesperson started doing just that: asking. No sales talk. No product benefit. Just, "Would you like to pick out a pair of socks? Would you like black (or brown) polish for those shoes?"

Now as professional salesfolk know, that's not the best selling job in the world—far from it. But would you believe sales of socks and polish jumped 50 percent in the stores insisting on this Ask and Get policy?

Did it cost anything? No. Did it take extra time? No. The customer was at the check-out anyhow. But it sure sold the product.

People will buy *if* you ask. So ask!

HUMAN NATURE EXPERT

One of the nation's greatest salesmen, Georgeson Hodge, once said he'd been too busy selling to learn much about salesmanship. This man was a millionaire. He may not have called it salesmanship. But he knew a great deal about human nature. Whenever he made a call, he always did exactly what I am advising you to do: he asked the customer to buy.

Many customers turned him down. They were not in the market. His prices were out of line. Hodge never talked back.

He was too shrewd. He would slowly pack his samples and reluctantly prepare to depart. Almost at the door, Hodge would turn back, and blandly and graciously ask the customer for his business. This he did, not as a beggar asking for alms, but as a friend asking a favor of another friend. His manner and request flattered his customers. Many, immediately after dismissing him, turned right around and gave Hodge an order.

Ask and Get, like the other closing techniques, is valuable only when practiced consistently. Asking one prospect to buy and then failing to ask the next three or four won't build your business. But asking every prospect to buy certainly will!

This is the seventh—and last—of the secret closing keys. Now you're ready for the special keys to round out your knowledge of closing sales.

A BAKER'S DOZEN OF
SPECIAL CLOSING KEYS

18

RUDYARD KIPLING gave this advice on how to compose a poem: "There are nine and sixty ways of constructing tribal lays, / And every single one of them is right."

Ditto with closing sales. Anything that works is good.

Thousands of successful salespeople use hundreds of closing methods. Some are soft sell—some hard sell. But one characteristic they all share in common is the willingness to try, try, try again.

Joe Bowlin of Fort Worth certainly has one of the most unusual methods. Joe always carries a Polaroid camera in a special pocket. When closing time comes, he sticks an order blank under the prospect's nose and says:

"I want to give you a picture doing the most important thing you did today."

It works.

A. H. Rosenthal, the great salesmanship scholar, told of a salesman who began to sob at closing time *because he was doing the prospect such a favor.*

By now you have about all the equipment to become an expert closer. All you need to do is get out and use your closing keys until they're second to breathing as a natural function in life.

You have seven major secret keys—the great motivators. But there are variations you need to know as well, so you'll have a full bag of closing keys, enough for any occasion. Here are a dozen special keys to add to your seven major keys. Use what works for you.

1. *GIVE A CHOICE, NOT A CHANCE.* This was first made famous by Elmer Wheeler, an original contributor to salesmanship. Instead of giving the buyer a chance to buy from you, give him a choice. Don't ask him *if* he will buy; ask him *which* he wants to buy. "Which color do you prefer?" "Would you like to pay for this in 30 days or 90?" "Shall we ship by truck or air?"

After all questions are answered, all voiced reservations resolved, it's time to assume the prospect is ready to buy. If you aren't 100 percent sure the prospect is ready to sign the order, instead of asking directly for it, ask for it in a roundabout way: "Would you like us to handle the financing?" "Let's choose the color you'd prefer." "What would be the most convenient time for installation?" A postive response to any one of these questions is almost the same as signing the order.

Of course, this key is a variation of two of your major keys: the Beyond Any Doubt and the Little Question Keys.

2. *PUT THE UNDECIDED BUYER ON THE SPOT.* Despite your best efforts, sometimes the buyer simply refuses to cooperate. Help such a buyer help himself by placing him in a position where it will be difficult not to say yes. Ask: "Do you want six dozen of these, or do you think you can use eight dozen?" The buyer is then almost forced to choose one or the other. Don't ask the buyer outright to buy or even to agree with you. Fire a pair of questions thus: "Do you want this in the large or the small size?" "How soon must you have delivery?" Confusion in the buyer's mind (you put it there) works in your favor. When he or she answers yes, he or she will buy.

3. *MENTION MONEY CASUALLY.* Money enters into every sale, of course. What could be more natural than closing

on a money note? Say to the prospect: "Is it cash or charge?" There is a cash discount, you know." Ivan Daughtery, of Elmira, New York, taught his salespeople to ask: "Do you want to pay for this by cash or check?" Sales increased.

4. *ASK HOW TO SPELL THE NAME.* The most charming word in the language is the person's own name. Wise closers use this fact in framing the name-spelling close. Ask: does the prospect want full name or initials? Does she use Ms., Mrs., or Miss? Few prospects can resist this.

5. *APPEAL TO PRIDE.* Paint a picture. Show the customer occupying a place of pride. Make it vivid: "Imagine how you will feel driving up in this new car."

6. *FUTURE DATING.* Sew up an order for the future. Your prospect is not ready to buy now? Try to pin down delivery three months or even a year from now. That's better than letting a competitor walk away with it.

7. *ONE MORE THING.* When you try to close and fail, pull another arrow from your quiver and say: "Oh, I almost forgot to mention something very important. If you place your order this month, you'll get one case free. You simply cannot afford to pass up a savings like that, can you?"

8. *DO SOMETHING SPECIAL.* Many buyers, believing they are center of the universe, will not buy unless they feel they're getting something special, a price no one else is getting, for example. This can be and usually is a trivial thing. But to certain buyers it locks up the sale.

"Since you are such a big buyer, Mr. Brown, I'll tell you what I am going to do." You outline something special. With some buyers this is the best technique of all. I recollect a buyer who told me that unless he got a price lower than anyone else it was impossible to do business with him. I showed him the list price and then quoted him a lower one—exactly the price I intended for him all along. He signed.

9. *PROS AND CONS.* With analytical buyers who have difficulty making up their minds, take out a sheet of paper and write the pros and cons of your proposition, side by side. Naturally, you favor the pros. But no whitewash.

You admit certain shortcomings, but more than offset them with the pluses. He wants evidence. Give it to him in full measure and he buys.

Bob Pachter is convinced that the most powerful closing weapon is logic. Bob uses Socratic syllogisms to convince the most stubborn of buyers.

"It must be clear to a man of reason," he says (and who can resist such flattery?) "that if such and such is the case, thus and so must be, as day follows night. Therefore, there's only one thing for us to decide—how soon do you want these books in your library? Will next Wednesday be soon enough?"

When the buyer starts asking questions about such things as delivery date, the color selection, how long the contract will last, how much installation will cost, and so on, he's probably doing it with one thought in mind: that he's going to buy. At that point it's up to you to tie the knot on the package.

10. *SUMMARIZE*. Summarize all your plus points, even to writing them down—"This is what you will get." It is impressive. The prospect sees an array of benefits marching toward him.

"What more is there for me to say?" you ask. "It's all here in black and white. You can't say no to an offer like this, can you?"

Gayle Freeland is a close-the-sale-oriented World Book sales manager in Memphis. She loves to hear prospects ask how her product compares with her famous competitor, Encyclopedia Britannica. Her strategy is *not* to knock her competitor's authority.

Once a prominent businessman asked her to come to his office to explain why her product was better than Britannica.

"Mr. Dixon," she said. "World Book is widely known for its value in educating children. On that point, it has no peer. So I assume what your concern is why World Book is better for adults?"

Dixon nodded.

"Well, Mr. Dixon," she said, "when you want to look up something in Britannica, it's there all right. I wouldn't pretend otherwise.

"But it's not easy to find. Why should you have to work

that hard to get it? After all, your time is valuable. World Book makes it easy. That's why World Book is better.

"After all, World Book has 60 percent of the global encyclopedia market. The other 40 percent is divided among all the others. There must be a reason.

"There's also a reason why I sell World Book. I could be selling Britannica. But we always had World Book when I was small. There's no way we could have done without it. I believe in World Book."

Thus you have it. A powerful side-by-side comparison. Sure the competitor is famous. Sure, it's authoritative. But there are people who believe in World Book. Maybe ease-of-access has something to do with it.

Dixon bought. Gayle Freeland proved that closing sales depends on the closer—not the fame of the product.

P.S. She closed *without* once mentioning price—yet her product is half the cost of her competitor. And she was talking to a prospect who could easily afford any product he wanted! Does her lack of emphasis on price give you a clue? It should!

11. *THE WHISPERING CLOSE.* A high-volume purchasing agent says his most effective supplier whispers at the moment of closing, as if letting the buyer in on a dark secret.

"I leaned forward—not wanting to miss a word," the buyer related. "The salesman continued to whisper. I continued to follow his words. Before I knew it, he asked me to buy. Before I knew it, I whispered I would!"

12. *THE SILENT CLOSE.* A sundries salesman demonstrated power of the silent close. From morning till night, this man (I swear it!) didn't say a dozen words. He merely showed merchandise. He pointed to this feature and that. He demonstrated. He let the goods speak for themselves.

Then he started writing up the order and inquired: "How many?"

Similarly, Bob Pachter is a strong advocate of the power of silence in closing sales. (He's also a power-talker with a well-rehearsed presentation.) As often as not, when he has completed his presentation, he takes out an order blank, marks an X on it, and says: "Here."

One word plus silence does it.

"Crowd them with silence and they will sell themselves," he explains.

There are your dozen special keys, enough to close any buyer that ever placed an order, if you use them right, consistently, and often.

13. *THE WHAT-IF KEY.* To give you a baker's dozen, let's add the *What-If* Key from Robert E. Baxter of Los Angeles. Says Baxter: "There is nothing so devastating in real estate as to get caught in the cross-ruff between a buyer and a seller. His story:

I got caught this way on my first commercial real estate sale.

Real estate is no different from other selling. Basic methods are the same. People are people with the same curiosity, fears, hopes, and habits.

My sad lesson cost me a big commission.

I had a three-story office building listed for sale. The owner wanted $155,000—$60,000 in cash. The property had a $40,000 mortgage on it. The owner offered to carry a second mortgage of $55,000. A lot of repairs were necessary for the air-conditioning system, plumbing, and parking surface out back. I figured if the owner wanted to sell *as is,* the property was overpriced by about $20,000. The actual market value was around $135,000.

For three months, I brought lookers to the property but got no offers. By this time, the owner was softening and beginning to feel he would never get a buying proposal. It had been advertised and promoted.

Then, one day I got an offer of $140,000 from a prospect instead of the $155,000 asked. Of this he'd pay $45,000 cash, not the $60,000. Further, he wanted the air conditioning and plumbing repaired. I had no idea if the seller would accept this. Air-conditioning repairs alone would cost him nearly $8,000. It would mean selling at less than market value by my reckoning.

I presented the offer and just about fell over when the owner said he'd accept, provided he split cost of air-conditioning repairs with the buyer. In effect, he was willing at $4,000 to take $6,000 less than the market. He was really anxious to sell.

I ran joyously back to the buyer and told him the good news. I was sure the sale was in the bag. It wasn't. It was out of the bag and I was out of a commission.

Why? Simply because the quick reply caused the prospect to think: "Boy! This owner really wants to sell. He came down in price right off the bat and on top of that agreed to nearly all of my other demands. I'll just hold out for the whole package including my demand that he pay all the costs of air-conditioning repairs. Maybe there's something wrong with this deal. Maybe there's something I don't see. He gave me no argument." The prospect didn't sign.

So I went back to the seller with the original offer and told him what happened. The owner made a counteroffer which he asked me to take to the prospect and he made a counteroffer to the counteroffer. Next I got a counteroffer to the counteroffer to the counteroffer. See what I mean?

Instead of running back and forth so quickly I should have let a couple of days go by before I took the owner's first counteroffer back to the prospect. In this way, the prospect would think the seller was going to be difficult to convince and make the deal look hard. Above all, I should have remembered to use a wonderful selling technique called *What If!*

When I went back to the prospect with the owner's agreement to accept his offer with only one condition, I should have taken my time and kept the owner's acceptance in my pocket. I should have said: "I am having a very tough time trying to get the owner even to consider your offer. He knows he has a good piece of property. He might lower that price a little but he balks at paying for repairs. If you are too strong in your demands, he may take the property off the market entirely as far as you are concerned.

"But Mr. Prospect, *What If* I got the price down to $140,000? *What If* I get the owner to pay for the plumbing and parking surface repairs, and split the cost of the air conditioning? I don't know if I can do it, but if I can, would you accept that?"

What If?

Of course, all of the time I have the exact agreement signed by the owner in my pocket.

This makes the buyer want the deal. He feels he may lose an opportunity. You are in an excellent position as an expert negotiator. The prospect must rely on you. The prospect not only doesn't think of asking for more. He is thinking he will be fortunate to get anywhere near what he originally offered.

So he would probably say: "Yes, I would accept that kind of agreement. See what you can do." Then wait a day or two before you bring back the owner's agreement which you had all along.

When the buyer signs, he'll feel he's a clever fellow who has driven a hard bargain.

What If you use this simple little technique the next time you get caught between buyer and seller in any field?

You will make the deal! That's what!

WHAT TO DO
WHEN ALL SEEMS LOST

19

SO FAR in this book, you may have thought: "We're treating the prospect as if he were a pawn on a chessboard to be pushed around at the salesperson's whim."

Prospects are not pawns. They're flesh and blood—often cantankerous, difficult, unreasoning, implacable, mysterious. Sometimes instead of yielding to your closing logic, they set up barriers. They won't buy.

There you are, feeling as useful as a side pocket on a pig, merely a conversationalist, and not a salesperson. That is your predicament until you learn how to retrieve the lost sale. A good closer can take an apparently lost sale and retrieve it, take a dead sale and fan the breath of life back into it, turn a prospect's flat *no* into a gratifying *yes*.

PERSISTENCE IS VITAL

The one vital factor in reviving dead sales is *persistence*. It has proved its mettle time and again. If you are positive enough, persistent enough, forceful enough in an acceptable way, the buyer will often buy—even if he or she fully intended not to buy. The buyer cannot help yielding to one of the weaknesses that affects us all. But unless your persistence is adroit and skillful and inoffensive, you may annoy the buyer and blow your chances of selling.

Too many salespeople believe that merely hanging on makes sales. It doesn't. Intelligent persistence makes sales. If you are *smilingly* persistent, you will not offend the buyer. If you submit new ideas, new reasons, and new arguments, it will intrigue the buyer.

Your prospect has just said she doesn't want to buy—with emphasis. She leaves no doubt: she means it. But are you, a wise salesperson, downcast? Not for a second. You know it doesn't mean the sale is lost. It only means you must sell harder. So you bring in new sales ammunition, new ideas, cascades of interesting new angles. Don't tiresomely repeat the same appeal. Say and try something new.

To pull the sale out of the fire, be prepared with both a primary and a secondary presentation—the first to win initial interest and to try to close, the second to stick with her when she decides not to buy. Launch a reserve attack when your first onslaught is turned back.

That little word *why* is an ace in the hole. Ask *why* the buyer believes such and such, *why* she isn't ready to buy. *Why* is a pleasantly persistent word. It pins the buyer down to cases—and then usually disarms her.

WHAT YOU DID WRONG

Joe Skinnerbaum, a $40,000-a-year salesman, always asks the no-buyer this question while packing up to leave:

"Mr. Carlson, would you mind doing me a favor?"

Usually the prospect says: "Not at all." We all like to do favors. Besides, in this case, the prospect feels the danger of buying is past. After all, isn't the salesperson packing up to go?

"Would you mind telling me what I did wrong?" asks Joe. "The fact that you didn't buy was my fault entirely, I am sure of that. I know you've decided against buying, so I am not going to mention that anymore. But if you'll tell me what my weakness is, it might help me talk to other prospects. **Believe** me, I'd appreciate it as a personal favor."

Two out of five of his buyers, by actual count, sell themselves in the process of telling Joe why they didn't buy.

Another way to retrieve lost sales takes more courage: turn the buyer's refusal into scorn and ridicule. Use it with great finesse or it'll turn against you. John Barnhart uses this technique in selling expensive books to women.

"It's the most effective way I know of snagging a lost sale," he said.

The woman says she decided not to buy. John says nothing for a while. He just stands there as if dazed at such an announcement. Then he says:

"Madam, you have just told me you are not going to buy these books for your children. Do you know what you're really saying? You actually said you're willing to let your children struggle on without every help you can give them. Who knows, you may be needlessly handicapping them in getting along in the world. You're telling me you're willing to let those children struggle against odds! When just ten cents a day would give them a better chance!

"But I don't think you meant that, Mrs. Johnson. It's a dime a day against the handicap of inadequate preparation. You ought to be willing to invest that to give those children a start in life."

Strong language?

"They don't seem to resent it, and it saves at least one sale out of five," John declared.

Mack Binney uses this same technique in selling office equipment. "No, of course you don't want this equipment," Mack says. "If you did want it, you'd be using it now. But, tell me, do you really know *why* you don't want it?"

Why again.

TELL A STORY

When the buyer says no with a steel eye, stop the action and tell a story.

Ellerbe Hobbson, one of the nation's master salesmen, supplies sales aids to retailers. The buyer, George P. Jones, has just told Hobbson he's decided not to buy.

"I am glad you're so frank, Mr. Jones," Hobbson says. "I admire a frank man. Besides, your conviction shows you've thought about what I was telling you, and are honestly convinced you do not need this service.

"That reminds me of the time I called on Abel Clemenson of Clemenson Motors. He brought up the same point. He's a Victory dealer same as you are. He has 18 people working in sales, a few more than you do.

"Mr. Clemenson said: 'Hobbson, I don't think my crew will read and apply your material.' Then he said, 'Just a moment, I see it's different from other services. I like its pocket size and indexing features. It gets right down to real problems. If only one idea gets across to one of my people, it'll make a big profit on my small investment.' Mr. Clemenson bought of his own free will.

"Two weeks ago, I dropped in on Mr. Clemenson. He said, 'Hobbson, I want to tell you I'm mighty glad I bought your service. I never thought they'd read or use it. But they can't wait for future installments. I don't mind telling you the profit on one sale made by my weakest salesperson will more than pay for this service for five years.'

"Now, Mr. Jones," concludes Hobbson, "what this service is doing for Mr. Clemenson, what it's doing for Mr. Grimm in Chicago, what it's doing for Mr. Hackett in Grand Rapids, what it's doing for all these organizations—it will also do for you. Will you just initial this form for me, please?"

The running narrative brings prospects around to buying, perhaps better than any other technique. The narrative revives the sale and closes it.

The good closer doesn't cringe when the prospect delays buying or decides not to buy. Recognize *no* for what it is—an excuse. Then get to work, overcome the excuse, circumvent it, rescue the sale, and close it!

"I'LL THINK IT OVER"

Really good closers make only one call per prospect. They don't think about callbacks. Bob Pachter says frankly to his prospect:

"We are going to decide this today. I won't see you again."

When Pat Barry hears, "see me later, I'll think it over," he sees it as a challenge.

"Most sales are made because you don't take the first 'come back later' seriously," Barry says.

"Your prospect is hesitant because he's undecided. Push his 'come back later' right into his face. Ignore it. Move in with a profit idea.

"Accept the challenge. Convince the prospect he cannot afford to wait. You can do this if you've analyzed his needs. Your prospect is interested in *his* needs—not yours.

"A genuine interest in fitting your product to his needs will prove you want him to benefit from what you are offering. If he continues to hesitate, keep showing him where it's to his advantage to buy now. Determine when you have aroused enough desire to make the sale."

"I'll think it over" is not an honest resistance. Refuse to take it seriously. Keep pushing, pushing, pushing until you get the order. That's what topnotch salesfolk the world over do.

ASSUME THE BUYER DOESN'T UNDERSTAND

Mark Wright is an energetic young seller of ad space in Newport News, Virginia. He closes sales by assuming the prospect didn't understand—never that he or she doesn't want to buy.

The buyer has just said *no* and is ushering Mark out. Mark stops him.

"I guess I didn't make it clear," Mark says. "I'm sorry. Now what this is—." He then starts his entire presentation from the beginning. Often that does it and Mark walks out with a signed ad order. Some buyers still say no. Patiently, Mark starts again at the beginning and goes into it all again. After three times, even the stalwarts falter.

"It's my fault," Mark says. "I should have been clearer. Now what we have—."

Doesn't he rub some prospects wrong? Theoretically, perhaps. But he's very well-liked. He sells a lot of ad space by assuming the buyer didn't understand and, once he does understand, will buy—naturally.

RESCUING THE LOST SALE

Would that every sale wanted to be closed! But some sales don't want to be closed. You know that. You must also know how to take such a sale, fan in the breath of life—and then close it.

But you and I know there are sales where everything goes wrong. Instead of being compliant, the buyer is stubborn. Rather than doing what she should do, she goes off on a tangent and upsets your plans. In place of saying *yes* when you try to bring the matter to a head, she turns you down flat.

To be a closing specialist, you must know how to handle conditions and prospects of all kinds.

The out-and-out refusal is a common experience. The buyer says *no*, and means it. In spite of all your knowledge of how to close, you draw a *no*. Your problem is to revive interest and get the buyer back on the track, to close in spite of the unwillingness to buy. How?

Often the best way is simply to refuse to hear the no. Go blithely on with your presentation. You've already learned it's important to assume you're going to close and carry that attitude right on through the sale.

If you ignore the *no* and keep right on with your presentation, something you say the second time may intrigue the buyer. Many times you can close after a definite rejection, provided you courageously get the buyer back into the picture.

Sometimes, however, the buyer will take your insistence as an affront. You reduce this risk if your demeanor remains professional.

If the buyer says a firm no a second time, it is usually a good idea not to ignore it any longer. The following are other ways to stay in the ball game.

APPLY THE BALK

In baseball, the pitcher walks up to the mound, goes through the motions of starting a pitch, stops midway, throws the ball to a base—trying to trap a runner. This is a balk.

In selling, you apply it much the same way.

The buyer says no sale, not once but twice, and that's that. An unwise salesperson argues, making the buyer more determined not to buy than ever.

The smart salesperson never runs that risk—but applies the balk. When the buyer says no for the second time, get to your feet and say:

"Well, you're the doctor."

Start packing samples. You appear to be in a hurry, which gratifies the buyer. The buyer knows as long as you're on the scene, he may buy something. Start for the door, put your hand on the knob, and then, as if you just remembered something important, say: "By the way," and launch into a subject far removed from the product or the sale—some subject, if possible, you know will interest the buyer. Before you know it, you've switched the subject back to business, and before long you're seated at the buyer's desk, unpacking samples!

THE SHOCK TREATMENT

Chuck Fears, a leading life insurance salesman, is indomitable. He often runs into a situation where the sale seems lost. Fears uses shock treatment.

"Before the prospect is ready for it, I flash an application and ask him to sign it," Fears says. "Quite taken aback by my rush, chances are he signs.

"Then I tell him it's not a contract until I have a check. I ask him for one. Usually he draws the line.

"Then I play my ace card: 'Here, you take this application blank. I want you to put it in your safe deposit with your own other valuables.'

"He wants to know why. My answer: 'So your wife can see how close you came to relieving her of all financial worries. So your children can see how close you came to providing them with a college education.'"

That usually does it. The prospect is glad to make out a check.

"I don't know how many deals I have closed this way," says Fears. "It must run into the thousands."

It does take courage to use a technique like that. But without courage, what right have you to call yourself a salesperson?

As that great American philosopher, W.C. Fields, said: "The time has come to grasp the bull firmly by the tail and face the situation squarely."

VALUE OF PURE REPETITION

A salesperson selling a special tool to oilfield construction crews called on one cantankerous man 19 times—no sale each time.

"Young feller, I'd like to know why you keep coming to see me since I never buy," the roughneck crew chief said.

The salesperson was firm but pleasant.

"That's why I keep coming back," he said. "And I'll keep on coming until you buy. I'm convinced you need this tool."

The prospect gave up.

"Holy Mother of Mercy!" he said. "I suppose you may as well send me a trial order. Looks like I've got no choice."

P.S. He's still using the tool—which turned out to be a boon on the job. Chalk up one for pure repetition.

ADMIT THE UNTHINKABLE

Irving P. (Swifty) Lazar, a legendary showbiz agent, is a lawyer by training—but describes himself as a salesman. In the 1950s, Lazar bet Humphrey Bogart he could close five deals for Bogart before dinner one day.

He did. Bogart paid up and gave Lazar his famous nickname—Swifty.

Says the diminutive Lazar:

"I'm proud to be the prince of pitch. I'm a salesman. When I'm in New York, I'm worried about who's selling what in Hong Kong. When I'm in Hong Kong, I'm wondering who's selling what in Moscow."

In selling book rights to publishers, Lazar takes a hard line:

"Before I go back to the Coast, I want a firm offer."

If the publisher turns him down, which happens even to a legend, Lazar voices the unthinkable:

"What's the worst thing that could happen, Mr. Publisher?" he asks. "The worst is we don't sign an agreement. You'll still be around. So will I."

By appearing offhand—in effect, saying who needs his sale anyhow?—Lazar whets the buyer's appetite. After all, if he's not eager to sell, does he have a competitive offer just as good? (In poker, veteran players say: "Scared money cannot win." The same holds true in selling.)

Lazar then bounces right back and starts talking about the values of his property. He's a champion closer. Now in his seventies, he appears to be in his prime.

"If you keep moving, you won't get hit with a hunk of pie with a brick in it," he says. "If you stop someone's going to get you. People who stand still are liable to get run over by people who don't."

COME BACK TO PROFIT

Pam Pearson is a dynamic saleswoman who offers decorative accessories to retailers in Texas. MaLeck, one of her manufacturers, recently named her salesrep of the year. Pam closes sales after other reps have packed up and left the retail fray.

One department store buyer was downright rude.

"I don't like your products," she said. "I'll never buy."

"Well, you may not, Miss Grimm," Pam said. "But the public does. So much so, they sell themselves."

"Humph!" said Miss Grimm and terminated the conversation.

Once a month, for the next 15 months, Pam Pearson called on Miss Grimm—each time with another story about how well MaLeck products were selling in such-and-such a store.

Finally, it became clear: personal dislike aside, it was not good business to ignore a product other stores were making money on. Miss Grimm placed her first order.

At last accounting, Miss Grimm had bought $113,000 worth of products in one year—and volume continues to rise.

"She's my largest customer today," Pam Pearson says.

When the buyer doesn't like the product, talk money—the universal favorite. It closes sales when all else seems lost.

HOW TO CLOSE
FOR KEEPS

20

THINK your work is finished when the buyer signs the order? It's not. One more vital step remains: nailing the sale down for good.

One-shot Finnegans are salespeople who close a sale once and never go back to the same customer. They don't wear well. They close by deception, too much pressure, misrepresentation, or they lose the confidence of the prospect in some other way.

One-shotters are not good salespeople. The man or woman who can make a sale, call on the customer later, and continue to increase the volume—here's the salesperson who makes big money and gets promoted to a better job.

Let's examine the road trod by salespeople who close for keeps—those who make a sale, make it stay closed, and call back and get more business, time after time.

Sales have a habit of reopening just when the salesperson believes everything is closed. The reopening is sometimes a cancellation, sometimes a reduced order, sometimes a postponement.

Your job is to close the sale and lock it tight with Post-Selling Techniques. Develop additional presentations for use after closing.

Realize what happens in the buyer's mind after he's been sold. For you, the close is a victory. You're elated. For the buyer, it's an uncertainty. Buying fears have been momentarily overcome. But now the fears come back.

The buyer thinks: "Did I make a mistake? Will I get my money's worth? Could I have done better elsewhere? Will these be what I really need? How do I know the firm is reliable? What will the stock market do? Am I going to lose my hard-earned money?"

As these fears start to work, they turn the buyer into a doubter. The same person who willingly signed your order now withers you with: "I've been thinking the matter over. Better hold up on my order for a while. There are some factors I didn't think of when I told you I'd buy. I'll call you."

This doesn't occur occasionally. It occurs often. It comes from the abnormal buying psychology of the buyer you've already learned about.

How to handle it?

DON'T LINGER

First, a good closer doesn't linger longer than absolutely necessary once the sale is closed. Get out. A fine salesperson recommended this formula. "Get in—get through—get out." That is good advice.

Get out as quickly as you can. But don't run like a fugitive. Obviously, leaving too fast arouses distrust and ill feeling. However, don't stay and engage in social conversation one minute longer than necessary. Don't give the buyer a chance to think about cancellation or postponement.

TWO BIG WORDS: THANK YOU

Express the most beguiling and valuable sentiment in taking leave: gratitude. Too many salespeople slur over this step, treat it as inconsequential, pay little or no attention to it. That is wrong. Thank the buyer cordially, sincerely, and warmly—even if you had to fight every step of the way for that order.

Say "Thank you!" and really mean it. Smile! Show the buyer you appreciate the business. We all want to be appreciated. We all like to feel our business is important and vital. We like to think our purchase keeps a department store operating, an insurance company in business, a steamship line running. Stoke the idea in the buyer's mind.

Bill Miller, a mobile home salesman, used this technique in keeping Joe Conforti, one of his dealers, sold.

"You're my biggest customer," he said to Joe. "I'm going to buy you a steak."

Joe Conforti was flattered. "I had no idea my business was that important," he said, beaming.

Small thing? Sure. But do you think any of Bill's orders were likely to come unglued?

Sometimes gratitude leads to amazing benefits. Lynn Doyle had been contracting only three months when he unearthed a large prospect. He made his approach. Only a youngster, it thrilled him that John B. Phillips would let him quote on a million-dollar project.

Lynn gave Phillips the best he had. But it wasn't good enough. The business went elsewhere. Naturally, he was discouraged but not beaten. He called Phillips and thanked him cordially.

"But what have I done for you?" John Phillips said. "I placed the business elsewhere."

"I know that," Lynn told him, "but you did more for me than you realize. You see, Mr. Phillips, you are the first big man who had enough confidence in me to let me quote on an important project. It was an enormous boost to me as a new company. I want to thank you. I am deeply grateful."

Nothing happened for three days. Then Phillips called Lynn Doyle over and gave him a contract for another building. The gratitude pleased Phillips. He expressed his pleasure by giving Lynn Doyle a different piece of business.

POST SELLING

Before you leave a closed customer, make a brief pointed reassurance talk. The shorter the better—the more pointed the better. Highlight the advantages. Tell your customer again of the profit and satisfaction he's going to get.

"I congratulate you on your choice, Mr. Wilsie," one salesperson says. "You will enjoy months and months of satisfaction from this equipment. And you will save money, too—the market is definitely headed upward. Thirty days from now it would have cost you $75 more to duplicate this model."

Or, as he leaves he says:

"Mr. Wilsie, to a man of your business judgment, I needn't even say this—but it's wise you're placing this order now. As time goes on, you'll be more and more satisfied." Then out he gets.

One retail clerk got the post-sell theory right but missed the application. Whenever a customer bought playing cards, the clerk said:

"Thank you very much. I hope you win with these."

"Thanks," responded one customer. "I just hope you don't say that to each customer."

"Sure I do," said the clerk, seriously, "the playing card company instructs us to say that. It makes customers feel lucky."

As all sales trainers know, you can't win them all. As the native New Yorker said to the tourist: "Radio City? It's easy. Watch me and get off two subway stops *before* I do." Oh, well.

ACQUISITION, NOT PURCHASE

Hubert Bermont* learned the value of selling for keeps when he trained in retailing. Says Bermont:

> When I was a young salesman, a top-notch colleague always went home with the biggest commission check. He

---

*From *How to Sell Yourself Successfully in Your Own Field*, by Hubert Bermont, Bermont Books, 815 15th Street, Washington, D.C. 20005. Used by permission.

had 30 years' experience. Having armed myself with product information as the old-timer had, I went into combat with customers: wheedling, cajoling, charming, telling jokes and even threatening them with consequences of not buying.

I was the good guy trying to make sales to support my new young family. They were the bad guys trying to prevent me from making sales. After each infrequent sale, I was emotionally exhausted.

Mr. Experience had no such days. He was easygoing, calm, and lost very few sales. One day, he took me aside and said:

"Kid, I like you. I'm going to explain why you have the wrong approach and the wrong attitude. These customers aren't your enemies. They don't wander in by accident or to come out of the rain. They come here because they want something.

"You act as if they're here to give you a rough time. As if it's your duty to remind them they came in to buy something. They have a genuine need for what we sell, but they're frightened. These are tough times. They work hard for their money. They are terribly concerned about buying something they don't need nor want.

"Your job is to calm them and help them part with money. Your job is not to fight them and try to grab their money because of your own needs. Their needs come first."

NAILING DOWN SALES WITH EMPATHY

Ellery Jordahl today is president of River City Furnace Ltd., Mason City, Iowa—the city known for flamboyant salesmanship as the fictional River City in *The Music Man*. But a greater contrast between Jordahl and Professor Harold Hill would be impossible to find.

Jordahl is low key and sincerely believes in supplying a quality product. He was his company's initial salesman for River City's Hot Shot furnace and remains the strategist behind all sales today. He believes in nailing down sales because he's selling for keeps. After all, his Hot Shots last ten years or longer. His first key sale was to Dave Wetzel in Waterloo,

Illinois. He wanted to establish Wetzel as his distributor for Illinois.

"The sale was memorable because at the time I didn't have a product to deliver," Jordahl recalls. "Yet I had to collect a $9,000 deposit on my word alone so I could start making it. I had never met Dave or Rita Wetzel face-to-face in my life. On top of that, they had never been furnace distributors before. So it was a new venture for them."

Formidable barriers, indeed! How did Jordahl approach it?

"At that time I was in the process of developing the Hot Shot woodburning furnace for homes," Jordahl says.

"I made them aware of the fact that I was going to be merchandising this product across the whole United States and that distributorships were going to be open on a state-by-state basis.

"I talked to Dave and his wife on the phone. I told them I'd bring down a Hot Shot prototype."

Jordahl drove from Eau Claire, Wisconsin, to Waterloo. He arrived at the Wetzel farm late one afternoon and had dinner with Dave and Rita. He took it slow. After dinner, he took the Hot Shot prototype out of the box.

"They were astonished," Jordahl says. "They'd never seen anything with such attractiveness and quality."

Again no rush. He told them he wanted a deposit of $9,000 for the Illinois distributorship.

The Wetzels wrote out the check. But Jordahl didn't consider the sale finished—far from it. He wanted to carefully nail it down—he was selling for keeps. He wanted to establish trust. He started emphasizing the area they both shared: farming. The implication: one farmer can trust another.

"I told Dave I was willing to give him a chance in a new field. He never had any experience and when I started out, I never had any experience either. I told him I was interested in him because I knew that farmers get up in the morning with the birds and they work until work is done. A lot of people are eight to five people and it's hard for them to be successful. I kept telling Dave why I had faith in him."

Jordahl kept talking for a couple more hours—nailing down the sale.

Today Wetzel is Hot Shot's largest distributor, accounting for 1,000 units a year. Wetzel has established 90 dealers in Illinois and Missouri.

"This was a permanent sale because I had faith in a customer and showed it," Jordahl says. "In return, they had faith in me. They actually wrote out a check strictly on my word. I make mistakes too. But usually I go by the first impression. Honesty makes people credible to me. And my honesty comes across to them. I don't know all of the answers but I know a lot of them. Like these people were farmers. We were talking in different ways about farming. He could tell I meant what I said because I did—and it showed."

Again, the master salesperson knows when to break the sign-up-and-get-out quick rule. When you're building a long-range relationship, consider staying longer to cement the tie—with empathy.

POWER OF INVOLVEMENT

Robert Connolly closes for keeps via customer involvement. The sale is nailed down because the customer comes to believe he made each critical decision along the way.

"When you convince the buyer the purchase plan is *his* idea, remarkable things occur," Connolly says. "Once he accepts credit for a procedure, he'll defend it. So he is convincing you and thus selling himself."

Sound exciting? It is. But, like most sophisticated sales principles, it takes time and practice to master.

How to credit your prospect? It may fall into place. You simply pretend it was his idea. React as if the idea had just occurred to you. Show a growing enthusiasm for his idea. Then he will start to sell you.

You might start the process with a statement: "You know, you really have quite an idea there."

Or a question: "What is your judgment on the best course of action here?"

This whole technique is based on human vanity. If your prospect believes your idea is his idea, he will defend it with honor to the end.

You're selling a line of commercial supplies. You write your regular size order, then ask:

"Do you feel it would be good planning to reserve an additional quantity for delivery during May? Of course, we will confirm before delivery."

After a yes answer, but before leaving your prospect, say:

"You know, I like your idea for planning future deliveries. It makes a lot of sense."

You're selling magazine subscriptions. After you feel you have made your basic sale, say:

"I'd like to get your judgment on this matter. Do you prefer the convenience of our automatic renewal service subject to your cancellation in advance?"

Then later you say:

"You've got a good idea there. We'll set it up just that way."

DON'T NEGLECT CUSTOMER

Use each customer as a source of additional business. Your job is not to make sales but to make customers. Keep in touch with the customer. Find out how the product's working. See that the customer is kept pleased and sold.

A shrewd businessman in Detroit once sat down and wrote out his business credo. The sale, said he, *starts* when the order is signed. After that the seller must see that the customer gets the utmost profit, satisfaction, advantage, and use out of the product. That man was Henry Ford I. That credo did extraordinary things to the small business Henry Ford headed. It will do wonders for you.

The sale is only truly closed when your customer knows how to use the product or service, when he is satisfied. Your job as a closing specialist: drop in on your customer within a reasonable time. See how it's working. If you cannot look in on him, write a letter. Ask if there is any further service he needs.

If you want to keep the customer, keep in touch. Customers resent neglect. One of the chief causes of lost customers is failure of the salesperson to follow the sale.

One veteran salesperson, asked for the most important principle of all, said: "Never forget a customer. Never let a customer forget you."

Closing sales is much more than merely delivering a presentation in a prescribed way. Your job is building customers—not sales alone.

WHEN THE BUYER
TURNS YOU DOWN COLD

21

SOMETIMES experienced sales-people get turned down cold in situations where a novice—not knowing better—will win. When all else fails, return in manner to those innocent days. It often works.

Tom O'Ryan is a legendary salesman in transit advertising. Today he's probably the best-known name in his industry. It wasn't always that way. Back when O'Ryan first started selling transit advertising, for instance, he was assigned a territory in Georgia and The Carolinas. O'Ryan will never forget his first prospect—a bakery famous for Craig's Honey Bread. On Monday, O'Ryan called on the president.

"Young man, we've never used your advertising, and we don't intend to start now," he said.

On Tuesday, O'Ryan was back with a smile—and a new advertising idea. No sale.

He came back Wednesday, Thursday, and Friday.

On Saturday, he arrived at noon. The proprietor was getting ready to close for half holiday. At this point, O'Ryan didn't even know all the advantages of his service.

"I've been taught to answer all sorts of objections to transit advertising," he said, spreading his sales literature on the table. "It's all in here somewhere. Anything you ask I'm sure we can find—even if I don't know the answer."

It was a naive statement. No experienced salesperson would have said it. Yet the baker looked at the literature, back at the determined O'Ryan, then sighed:

"Well, this looks like something I'm going to have to have. Reckon you'd better sign me up."

O'Ryan wrote up his first customer.

"After that, I started *selling* advertising," O'Ryan said. He soon turned his Irish brogue into a plus. People remembered him. He became a distinctive personality and sell he did. Soon, O'Ryan ranked number one in the nation. He didn't know novices aren't likely to lead the pack.

"Nobody explained the averages to me," O'Ryan recalled. "I tried to sell one contract a day. I thought that was expected."

Ace salesman or not, O'Ryan always retained some of that early innocence. It's a good quality to go back to when you get a turndown.

Ask the buyer what you need do to sell him. Ask what benefit you should be stressing. Be naive. It closes sales.

VALUE OF PERSISTENCE

Even though he's an ace closer, Jim Halbert gets turndowns which he cannot, then and there, turn into a sale.

He called on one bank every week for eight years without getting an order. Eight years is a long time in any salesperson's life. But Jim thought it worthwhile to keep right on calling, keep right on trying to close.

Finally, he closed the sale. And the order—his largest—made up for the time he invested during those eight years. It also reflected his judgment: he knew this prospect was worth keeping on his active list.

Some would have quit at the end of a year. More at the end of two or three years. But Jim kept right in there.

If this were an unusual case, I wouldn't mention it. But most good salespeople can show you customer names sold only after repeated calls.

When the buyer turns you down cold, you face the true test. After all, anyone can be in good spirits when sales are closing the way they are supposed to close. But sometimes they don't. Remember the advice of John W. Gardner:

"The prospects never looked brighter. The challenges never looked greater. Men and women who are not stirred by *both* those statements are probably too tired to be of much use in the years ahead."

It takes uncommon courage to keep right on calling and get nothing but turndowns. But good salesfolk do it. They know it pays off. The important point: make your callbacks in the right way.

NOTHING TO LOSE? GET DRASTIC!

George Garmus believes in drastic action when you've been turned down, when there's nothing to lose.

"Why not?" says George. "You've already lost the sale. A drastic step just might shock the buyer into action. At the very least, you're no worse off."

George had been calling on Walter Hogan for several months. Walter needed George's product but he never would get off the telephone long enough to talk turkey. He had a classic case of telephonitis.

George walked in one day and Walter asked him what he wanted.

"Just a few minutes of your time," George said.

"Can't do that," Walter said, reaching for the telephone. "I've got to keep things humming around here."

He dialed a call. It was a clear turndown, similar to other clear turndowns. This is it, George said. Now or never.

He waited until Walter finished the call. Then he grabbed the telephone, dialed the company switchboard, and said:

"Please hold Mr. Hogan's calls until further notice."

Walter was aghast. George took control.

"Walter, three months back, we had a meeting like this— and I never did get a chance to tell you about this product. You bought another brand and I happen to know it didn't work near as well. That was *your* day. Today's *my* day. Will you agree to that?"

Walter, feeling undressed without his telephone, agreed—but looked at his watch. George then outlined the product benefits in a short fact-filled presentation.

"Okay, George, you win," Walter said. "We *should* try it. Now can I have my telephone back?"

George shook his head.

"Not until you sign this purchase order," he said. "I don't dare let you get on that telephone again."

Walter signed the order.

"It's a good product," he said. "I just wish I'd heard about it before."

That was one comment George decided he should *not* answer. After all, he had the order. He'd rescued a lost sale.

"Little drastic all right," George said later. "But I wasn't getting anywhere the other way. It worked."

When you don't have anything to lose, you may as well try a drastic step.

LEARN SPECIFICS FROM TURNDOWNS

You've done your level best to close—utilizing all your skill, forcefulness, and persistence. You've employed the closing secrets that apply to the case. But the prospect still won't buy. For reasons revealed or kept from you, the buyer simply will not budge.

Either you have failed to convince or the buyer lacks the ability to pay. Maybe there are some hidden reasons. No matter. No sale. If it's lack of ability to buy, you can do little. If it is some other reason—lack of conviction or something else—you must do something to try and close the sale.

First, review the sales conversation in your own mind. Determine where you fell down. Analyze the sale step by step and you may be able to tell where you lost control of the interview. Perhaps you didn't tell a complete enough story. Perhaps you failed to develop desire before you tried to close.

Several common faults prevent salesfolk from closing as many sales as possible. Know these five faults so you can avoid them:

1. *Being too eager.* Buyers resent that. Buyers like to feel they are doing the deciding. When an overenthusiastic salesperson goes too fast, they resent this much pressure and refuse to buy.

2. *Waiting too long.* You've already learned a premature close is better than waiting too long. If you delay your close, the buyer may cool. It sometimes takes superhuman strength to rekindle a cooled-off buyer.

3. *Your method was wrong.* Because you misjudged your buyer or his temperament, you used the wrong closing technique.

4. *Your foundation wasn't properly built.* You tried to close before any closing technique, no matter how fundamentally right or perfectly rendered, could close the sale.

5. *You misjudged your buyer altogether.* Some buyers are tricky. They sit and nod and give every evidence of being ready to buy. This is an act they perform for all callers. You reach for a close and you're thrown for a loss. But it can be surprising.

Review the sale in your mind to see if one of these five faults tripped you up.

ONE MORE ROUND

Now it's time to rebuild the sale. See if you can bring your prospect to the closing point once more. Don't give up without a fight.

James J. (Gentleman Jim) Corbett's answer to the question "How does a man become a champion?" is a good lesson in salesmanship. Said the heavyweight champion: "You become a champ by fighting one more round."

Fight one more round with your tough buyer. Try again to close with one of your closing keys.

Then if you simply cannot close, say goodbye in the most advantageous way possible. Be a fine sport. You are disappointed, of course. But don't show it. You are vexed. Don't show it. You are mad clear through. Don't show it.

Instead, follow Walt Whitman's sage advice: "Let your soul stand clear and calm." Smile. Show the buyer you are as big in defeat and in disappointment as others are in victory.

Always leave the door open.

Thank the customer for his time. He thinks he did you a favor by granting an interview. Tell him he did. Tell him sincerely that you enjoyed talking with him. Ask permission to call back at a later time. If he grants this (and chances are he will) when you do go back (and you *will* go back) you'll be an invited guest. This gives you a much better entree than you had the first time; it adds to your self-assurance. You will probably make the sale.

KEEP CALLING

If you don't make it the second time, keep calling until you do. The master secret of closing sales is to keep on calling, calling, calling. Keep trying to close!

Research shows that 80 percent of buying occurs after the fifth call. We also know that 80 percent of salespeople quit calling *before* the fifth call! To get more than your share of business, keep on calling and trying to close—it's that basic.

It is almost always too soon to stop calling upon a prospect. Today he or she might seem dead. Conditions change. Time works surely and steadily in favor of the salesperson who keeps returning. The need that didn't exist today may be a live and pressing demand tomorrow. So keep on calling—and closing.

Each time you call, try to close. A social call and chitchat may be pleasant. But it's not a sales call. You are only selling when you're trying to close. In between calls, maintain contact with your prospects and customers—a letter, a telephone call, anything that keeps you in touch. These contacts build confidence—the priceless ingredient in making sales. See your buyer as often as you can. In between times, don't let him or her forget you. Keep in touch the way you do with a friend you like, respect, and admire.

In salesmanship there's nothing more important than reacting to a turndown with grace and good sportsmanship. Leave the door open. If the buyer doesn't sign this time, there is always a next time. And another next time after that. Keep on calling and trying to close.

DON'T BLAME THE BUYER

When you call back, don't refer to your previous failure—as Kurt Wiggins did. Kurt tried to sell Brook Turner office equipment. Brook had a perfectly logical reason for not buying at the time. Two months later, Kurt Wiggins called and tried to make a sale again.

"You will remember, Mr. Turner, that I tried to sell you this once before, but didn't make the grade," began this inept salesman. "So I called today to see if I would have any better luck."

Well, he didn't.

A good salesperson never does it that way. Instead, rebuild the sale in your mind. Try to point out your own errors to yourself. Then correct those errors.

You may decide the closing technique was wrong for this prospect. Try to hit upon a technique that will be right and use it.

The most successful salespersons in the world make amazing records by rebuilding—the sure route to closing more sales!

BACK TO BASICS

When you get turned down, it's time to go back to basics. After all, when you're closing sales right and left, there's no need to review fundamentals. When its working, keep up the momentum. But when sales aren't closing, despite your best efforts, it's time to review the block-tackle-run side of selling—the indispensable cornerstones that make it all work.

Walter H. Johnson, Jr., chairman of Quadrant Marketing Counselors, Ltd., New York, is widely known as a sales speaker. He's also former president of Sales and Marketing Executives International. Johnson calls this back-to-basics review a "return to sharp-thrust selling," the skeleton of good salesmanship that whets the cutting edge of buyer motivation.

"The ability to sharpen your thrust makes the difference between losing and closing sales," Johnson says.

You sharpen your selling thrust by using timeliness, demonstration, research, alertness to trends, and pure selling power as tools, Johnson says.

"Put power into your selling effort," he advises. "Know and understand sources of selling power.

"Knowledge is power. Knowledge of your product. Knowledge of your prospect's needs. Knowledge of how to bridge the gap between the two. This power is developed by experience, analysis, and concentration.

"Confidence is power. Confidence in yourself. Confidence in product quality and value. Confidence in your ability to meet the customer needs.

"Expression is power. Mastery of words is essential in influencing others. When you face a customer, your ability to speak is crucial. Know the emotional power of words. Dress up your ideas with colorful, descriptive words. Develop power of expression by reading, practicing and collecting powerful words and phrases.

"Being affirmative is power. Prospects respond to a positive attitude and a can-do presentation. This is developed when you have pride in your product and when personal attitude is positive."

Basic? Sure. But many lost sales trace back to a lack of these fundamentals. When you get a turndown, it's time to go back to block, tackle, and run.

TURN ON EMPATHY AND CLOSE MORE SALES

22

NO SALESPERSON ever became great without learning how to use *empathy*. It is the secret of human relations in salesmanship. Its meaning is simple: *the complete understanding of another's feelings and motives.*

When you are empathic, you understand the prospect's feelings and motives, so you can address yourself in his or her terms. Let me show you what I mean.

PAUL MEYER'S SECRET

A man got up to give a presentation before a group. His fine reputation as a public speaker and salesperson had preceded him. I was in for a treat, I told myself.

What a letdown! The man couldn't talk at all. He hemmed and hawed, he groped for words, he stammered. But a strange thing happened to the audience. Instead of criticizing him or being disgusted with him, everyone tried to help the poor fellow discover the words. We all found ourselves helping him to make his speech!

He wanted each listener to invest $250 in a home study course. Inside of half an hour each did!

It was a masterful strategy in handling people. After the meeting, in private conversation, the master—Paul J. Meyer, of Waco, Texas—revealed his secret. It is the secret every salesperson must learn and use! *Empathy.* You need it every day in convincing others to like you and do what you want.

According to Meyer: "When I grope for words and you try to help me, we are doing something together. That is what empathy means. I do not want to shine, sparkle, be smarter than the folks in my audience.

"I want them to think they are brighter, smarter than I am. Then they will want to help me. That is what I want."

It's no trick. You are merely employing the secret weapon of asking (even though unspoken) the other person to do you a favor—rather than doing him one. It works in nearly every human situation. Try and you'll find out.

GETTING THE MAN RIGHT

Another man walked into my office. I knew I was in the presence of a master salesman—yes, and a master personality as well. He radiated self-confidence and success. He was a man, I felt sure, nothing could daunt. I got the feeling he had always been that way. He was, I decided, one of the lucky natural-born salesmen, destined from boyhood to attain success. He fascinated me with his engaging manner, by the easy way he presented his wares. I envied him, as we all envy those with such personalities.

We became well-acquainted. He was easy to know and natural to like. I complimented him upon his grace, personality, poise—his aura of success.

"Most of us struggle for years to gain what's natural with you," I told him. "I envy you being born with such gifts."

"Why, if you only knew what I was up until two years ago," he said. "A dismal failure—that's what. I tried a dozen different things and with a dozen different things I bombed out. I was a complete and total failure. I tried ten years to sell and flopped at everything I touched."

What brought about the change? He seemed reluctant to tell me.

"It sounds so silly I don't often tell it," he said. "But if you like, I will."

Two years before he was eking out a living in selling. He was often actually hungry. One night he stopped in a cheap hotel in a small Kansas town. After a scanty dinner, he sat in the lobby reading and watching baseball. He had no TV set in his room.

"That seedy lobby was an unlikely place to get inspiration, but that's where I got it," he said. As he slumped in a shabby chair, he watched a TV evangelist. The salesman was tempted to change channels—he wanted baseball. But something about the preacher's voice held him. He was telling a story: a father hoped to develop his gifted son into a mental wizard.

The boy was too young to read. The father brought jigsaw puzzles—each puzzle more difficult—to develop the lad's mind.

One night Dad brought home the largest and most difficult puzzle yet—intricate cuttings, a myriad of pieces. It was a map of the world. He told his son:

"Do this puzzle in a day and I'll give you five dollars. If it takes two days you get only one dollar."

"Okay, Dad," the boy said and went to work.

Inside of 15 minutes he was back, the puzzle completed. Each piece fit perfectly. The astonished father asked:

"Son, how did you get the complicated world map done so soon?"

"That's easy, Dad," the boy said. "The front side is a map. I looked on the back. It's a picture of a man. So I worked on *getting the man right*. Once I did that, I knew I'd get the world right."

And that, the salesman said, was the most important lesson of his life.

"It struck me like a ray of white light," the salesman said. "Get the man right, and you get the world right. If I got my man—my customer—right, I'd have my world right. So I resolved to make more sales by getting the man right.

"The next day I paid more attention than ever to my customers and prospects. I studied them. I tried to please them. From that day forth, the antagonisms I thought were built into selling (bickering, disappointments, misunderstandings) all disappeared. It was a new world. A world I'd dreamed about but never expected to see.

"That's the true secret of success—in selling and in life. Get the man right! Then you'll get the world right!"

PLAYING TO EGO

The closing techniques in this book work best when you get the man right first. Use the methods in tune with your prospect's desires and in keeping with his or her ideas.

Before it's anything else, salesmanship is the great art of pleasing people, particularly one person—your prospect. Few of us buy from a salesperson we dislike. We turn down a bargain if it means buying from an unlikeable salesperson. Think about the last person who slighted you, rubbed you the wrong way, or violated your precious ego. *Ego* from Latin means *I* or *self*. Most people are naturally afflicted with what one salesperson appropriately calls "I-trouble." Bear this human frailty in mind. Build on it in closing sales.

One woman used ego power to build a successful business. She was a widow, without money, with no business experience. She didn't want to leave her young son during the day. So against advice of friends and advisors, she went into business.

She had special knowledge of only one thing—antiques she had collected as a housewife. Taking a few pieces at home as stock, she rented an old house on the highway and opened shop. Her friends gave her six months to go broke.

Six years later, she had expanded 100 times. Her reputation was nationwide. How did she succeed? She learned to harness customers' egos.

"I soon discovered not to talk about myself, but to get them to tell me about themselves," she related. "Nine out of ten customers, with just a little persuasion, sold themselves—if I let them talk. They were pleased to show off their knowledge. They liked what they told me about my antiques so much they bought them!

"Eventually I worked out a selling technique called 'Feeding the Ego.' When a customer comes in, I show him a piece, make a few comments, and then ask him what he thinks about it. He usually rises to the occasion grandly and talks about antiques. He is proud to show off his knowledge. I am glad to listen. In the process of telling me about my wares, the prospect gets a much better estimation of himself, of the merchandise, and of me. My business relationships are marked by pleasant friendships and good profit. I feed the ego of my customers."

To make your closing techniques most effective, tie into your prospect's ego. Follow the sage advice of Abraham Lincoln in explaining his success as a lawyer:

"Whenever I am getting ready for an argument with a man, I spend two-thirds of my time thinking of him and of what he is going to say, and one-third of my time thinking of myself and of what I am going to say."

Follow that system. Keep the ego of your prospect in front as a perpetual guiding light. You'll sell more and sell easier. Ego is the cornerstone of human relations.

OPENING THE CLAM

What about the prospect you cannot get to talk? You can talk to The Clam, but he doesn't talk back. He just looks at you. This disturbs you. You lose your poise and you fail to make your sale. But The Clam can be opened easily and successfully if you play on that powerful force—the ego.

Appeal to the The Clam's vanity by drawing a picture where he plays a main part. He'll respond by becoming a great talker. One of the most difficult tight-lipped clams I ever saw simply would not talk. I gave him the sales story. He was as immobile as The Sphinx. It was demoralizing. One day I said to him:

"If there is anything I admire in a man it's taciturnity. When I am with you, I am talking to a thinker. You don't talk, talk, talk all the time—and I like that. Would you mind telling me how you developed such a magnificent gift of silence?"

That is pretty strong language. I didn't know if he'd throw me out. I didn't much care—I wasn't getting anywhere anyhow.

For the first time since I had known him, he began to talk. He talked well, once he got started. He explained why it was foolish for people to talk all the time. Silence was an obsession with him, he said, as he talked on and on.

Three years later he was still talking every time I saw him. Later I had a hard time getting away from him. I had appealed to his ego by complimenting him upon his silence.

What worked on this man might not work on others. Still, the principle is the same. If you can make The Clam the central figure, he will no longer be a clam. Talk about his hopes, his aspirations, his business, his problems. Compliment him judiciously. Ask his advice upon minor matters. Encourage him to drop his mask and become human.

EMPATHY WITH CHATTERBOX

Other prospects talk all the time and so fast that you can't get a word in edgewise. This prospect talks about everything under the sun. You find yourself talked out of the office before you even get near the closing point.

The principle behind handling him is exactly the same— namely, appeal to his ego. Direct the conversation to himself, an interesting subject for him. Then lead the conversation onto use of your product, giving him a chance to sell himself. Let the talker talk. Encourage him to talk. Compliment him upon being an interesting conversationalist. Then direct his thoughts onto the right subject, which is his purchase. Take this tack:

"You said something a minute ago that appealed to me, Mr. Mason."

He wants to hear what it is; he likes to have his own words quoted. Pause for an instant, then say:

"You said you believed everyone ought to make some provision for the perpetuation of his business."

He: "Yes."

You: "I don't need to tell you, Mr. Mason, that I agree, as every sensible person must. Now that is just where our proposition fits in with your picture." Then go into what you're selling.

From there on pick up the sales talk and keep it directed into relevant channels. Use of this vanity technique, appealing strongly to the prospect's ego, will banish other thoughts from the prospect's mind, and give you a clear field to bring about a close.

LISTENING CREATES EMPATHY

Dr. Kenneth B. Haas* believes the art of listening is the most powerful—and probably least fully utilized—tool in closing sales. Keep the ratio of one mouth and two ears in mind, he says. Listen twice as much as you talk.

"There are very good reasons for more use of ears in selling," Dr. Haas says. "Persuasion and motivation of people through asking questions and listening is the best way to bring prospects over to your viewpoint."

Good listening, Dr. Haas says, can be used to:

- Persuade, motivate, guide
- Control a prospect's purchasing activities
- Inflate the prospect's pride
- Learn his needs
- Remove obstacles
- Guide the prospect's thinking

"Listening and questioning carry equal weight," he says. "When both are used with skill, they become conversational selling—a rich and subtle art.

"Conversational selling stimulates intangible gains: customer goodwill, enhanced reputation, and the grand personal feeling that comes from selling like a professional."

Conversational selling may seem awkward at first. For decades sales managers have been emphasizing talking. Yet practical psychologists know that being a listener is often more important.

"Many times the prospect would have talked himself into buying if the salesman had listened more and talked less," he

---

*See Acknowledgments at front of book.

says. "When words flooded the prospect's mind, he became confused and doubtful."

Listening places you in your prospect's frame of reference. You demonstrate your appreciation and understanding of his or her feelings, attitudes, emotions, conflicts, and problems. Attaining empathy through questioning and listening is tough but profitable. You must be more alert, aware, and sensitive then you ever thought possible. Break out of your shell. Experience the mental and emotional status of your prospect.

Why is listening difficult? Because you:

- Fear losing the trend of the conversation
- Fear possible rejection
- Jump ahead in thinking
- Try to frame what to say in reply
- Fail to hear what's *behind* the words
- Forget to watch gestures that accompany your prospect's statements

Listening is a priceless asset. Listen for a moment after making each point to:

- Give the prospect time to digest it
- See if the presentation is clear
- Think ahead and organize the next step

"Listen with close and rapt attention," Dr. Haas says. "A talking customer is a helping customer. An average salesperson can become outstanding by adding more questioning and listening to presentations."

EGO WITH GROUPS

The ego technique is especially valuable in selling a board, a committee, or a group. Many expert salespeople fear group selling. This is a serious handicap. These days groups are more and more passing judgment upon important purchases.

Selling to a group is just as easy as selling to an individual if you always keep that dominant human factor—the ego—in mind. Appeal in the right way to egos of the group. Even more important, don't deflate the ego of any member.

You're meeting with directors of a company, trying to sell a costly installation. Find out beforehand the dominant personality on that board. It may be the chairman or president, but not always. The president and chairman may be figureheads. When you make your presentation, pay a little more attention to that dominant person. He will expect that attention. If you do not give it to him, you won't make the sale.

On the other hand, do not ignore any member of the group, even the secretary who keeps the minutes. One enemy on a board can kill the sale. Keep each member in the picture by appealing strongly to his or her ego.

How? Glance around the room, Catch the eye of each person and engage it momentarily as you talk. Address a sentence or two to each, looking at him as you talk. Then shift your glance to another. Never ignore these Look Compliments. Look slightly longer and more often at the dominant figure. Be sure you mention the name of each member at least once during the presentation. For example: "This is a field in which Mr. Wilcox has done a great deal of study. I am sure Mr. Wilcox's experience tends to support our conclusions in the matter."

Try to mention the dominant person *more* than once.

SMILE POWER

You can appeal to your prospect's ego without a single spoken word. Smile.

The salesperson who does not smile, does not please. Every salesperson could learn to use this important technique better. It unquestionably increases chances of closing sales.

Suppose the worst has happened—your prospect tells you he isn't going to buy. At this point, smiling is the last thing you feel like doing. You feel let down, whipped, irritated. But you can't show it. Smile. That tells more eloquently than words that you appreciate his point of view and understand his decision. It indicates good sportsmanship, which even the most unreasonable of buyers appreciates. That smile disarms the buyer. But it does something more: it gives you a chance to cover up your real emotions until you can decide just how to reply.

The sales manager of a large New York concern once assembled his salesforce to meet Jay B. Iden, leading Broadway director. He had engaged Iden to teach his salesfolk how to smile!

Iden took 500 persons one by one, rehearsed their best smiles, criticized them, pointed out errors, and embarrassed them. Many salespeople thought they knew how to smile, since they smiled each day on the sales firing-line. But this specialist in communicating human emotions pointed out: what they thought were smiles were *smirks*.

A smile wins goodwill. A smirk destroys it. The eyes make the difference. In a true smile the eyes also smile. In a smirk, only the mouth does. The eyes may continue to be hard, harsh, unfriendly.

After two weeks in smile clinic these salespeople went out and increased sales 15 percent. The right kind of smile will make your job surer, more effective, and will help you close sales.

O. C. HALYARD: EMPATHY EXPERT

O.C. Halyard, Jr., a crack real estate salesman and sales trainer, is an expert on empathy. His entire presentation is designed to build empathy with the prospect. In many cases, he uses prospect questions to build toward an empathic close. Says Halyard:

> *The Sincere Buyer* will have questions that are often buying signals. Remember, people criticize what they like. Use these questions to build empathy.
> The prospect asks: "Is the seller leaving the drapes?" This is a buying signal. Ask: "Would you like to have the drapes?"
> Prospect: "When will the seller give possession?" Answer: "When would you like possession?"
> Objection: "The rooms are too small." Answer: "You think the room is too small?" Your buyer may answer: "Yes, but I guess it isn't that bad." The fact that you don't have the same feeling helps convince him it's really not an objection.
> If the objection is illogical, don't disagree. Say: "I

understand how you feel, Mr. Jones, but have you considered this?" Above all, don't argue with the prospect. Even if you win, you lose.

Convert objections to benefits. For example:

- "The small property will be a lot easier to maintain, the taxes will not be as great, resulting in more leisure time and money saved."

- "I know you would have preferred larger bedrooms. However, this home is typical of this price range. Most families require maximum space in the family room and kitchen as we find here. This is where most of our day is spent. In order to be in a location as desirable as this one, we must consider the benefits of the size of the other rooms."

A price objection to $500 will not seem as large once you convert it to a per day or per week investment.

After a showing, sit with the prospects in the most comfortable room in the house and discuss the home. Then give the prospects an opportunity to talk privately.

Many salespeople talk themselves out of sales. Instead, listen to the prospect, ask good questions to guide his decision. Let him help sell himself.

When he is agreeing with you, give him the opportunity of confirming his own decision. Don't interrupt. Show interest with an occasional nod. If he pauses, sit quietly, allow him to organize his thought. Answer questions briefly without bringing up new items. When he indicates he is sold, get his signature.

Your trial-close asks for an opinion. Take the prospect's buying temperature before you ask for the decision. Ask questions on minor points where you expect a positive response.

- "In your opinion, Mrs. Jones, do you feel the kitchen has adequate table space?"

- "In your opinion, do you feel this yard offers the privacy you want?"

Use the word *feel* rather than think. We do not want them to go into deep thought. We simply want their emotional reaction. Then when the buying temperature is warm, close.

Note how each step in Halyard's presentation is designed to prove his understanding of—and sympathy with—the prospect's needs and opinions. When you build this much empathy as you go along, closing the sales is a logical final step.

THE PAUSE TO CLOSE

Often the most dramatic happening in a stage play is the strategically placed pause. Sometimes the white space in an ad is more eloquent than the large headlines. In selling, the pause—the block of silence—often closes the deal.

The pause enables you to control the interview as nothing else can. It helps you unpoise the buyer. It helps you recover your own poise if the buyer catches you off guard. Silence is a powerful influence in controlling others.

You've been trying to close a buyer and he has turned you down. His objection is specious and you know how to answer it. Instead of answering, you pause. Say nothing. Look at him, smile, and remain silent. The pause gives you an advantage over the buyer. He will be unpoised. Few can stand silence. He'll be wondering what you are going to say. This gives you an advantage when you start to talk.

Your silence also compliments him in a mild way—you take time to think before you start to answer his objection. It shows him you consider his objection valid enough to be thought out carefully.

When there is occasion for an explanation, or when the buyer asks for your advice, you have an opportunity to use the pause. The pause requires courage. Silence, as an aged and wise philospher said, is a tremendous weapon—if you have the willpower to use it. Practice until you can use the pause without difficulty, until it becomes second nature. You can control the buyer with your silences quite as effectively as with your words. The correct use of the pause will go a long way toward helping you closing sales.

THE PEOPLE BUSINESS

If you *get the man right*, everything else about selling will be right. In the final analysis, salesmanship will always be the art and science of understanding and controlling human nature. If you get the human side of any job right, the closing techniques in this book will attain their most effective use.

What about the so-called science of character analysis? A great deal of misinformation has been peddled about this "science," and it has done salesmanship a great disservice.

Don't try to be a good judge of character. Do not try to prejudge anyone, or like or dislike anyone on that basis. Try to sell everyone you talk to. As you come to know your prospect better, you naturally will learn what manner of person he or she is—that is, character.

Besides, what difference does character make if the person is a legitimate prospect for your product?

Modern psychologists say that there never was a "science" of character analysis—only a glittering pseudoscience.

SHORTER CALLS EQUAL MORE CLOSES

Want to increase your closing percentages? Make more *short* calls, fewer *long* calls. It is as simple as that. Don't dismiss it because it is so simple.

A sales trainer, spending a week in the field, found more than *half* of the calls were *unduly* prolonged by salespeople. They lingered. They told stories. They visited. They didn't want to leave.

You should get through with the presentation as soon as you can, eliminate small talk and chatter, try to close, and then pleasantly and unhurriedly get out.

The buyer for one large chain won't talk to salespeople if they don't have anything new to say or show. But if there's something new in packaging, cost changes, new products, things like that, he's glad to listen. He discourages lunch with salespeople as a waste of time.

"Ninety percent of buyers aren't influenced by lunch anyway," says he. "Most buyers can afford to buy their own lunches and would prefer to."

During the interview he wants the salesperson to eliminate small talk entirely.

One great salesperson made it a point to be the first to rise in every interview. He got in, said what he had to say, got on his feet, and got moving—he was an outstanding salesperson.

GIVE MORE TO SELL MORE

James Mangan developed the idea of selling by giving.

"In American industry, men make from $40,000 to $10 million a year at selling," Mangan said.

"To a man, they have all been givers. A giver gives the prospect something. He is not a Santa Claus, nor a philanthropist. He is just a giver.

"Give—and you will surely sell."

If you can't give money or cut prices, then what?

Give the gift of attention. Is he talking? Listen. You learn by paying attention.

Give the gift of praise. You love praise. So do others. Then why not praise the prospect?

Give the gift of consideration. Perhaps this is the greatest gift. Through consideration you put yourself in the prospect's place. Ask yourself: "If I were this person how would I feel toward me?"

How simple are these gifts. Yet how valuable in closing sales. How effective in demonstrating empathy for your prospect.

POWER WORDS
THAT CLOSE SALES

23

WHETHER you close sales on your first call (as Bob Patcher does) or you pay the price of repeat calls for years (as Jim Halbert did) the one force that brings you orders is *words*.

Words sell. Since we all use words in selling, there must be certain words that have more motivating power than others—power words. So let's learn the power words for closing sales.

You now have tested closing keys, proved and established. The nation's greatest salespeople use these techniques to become infinitely better, more successful, more prosperous. If you study, master, and use these major and special keys only one thing can result: more sales.

These closing techniques can be properly used or misused. They can be effectively or ineffectively applied. Often your *manner* in using the technique is more important than the techniques themselves.

Power words, tested on the sales firing line, can make your closing keys most effective because they drastically improve your manner.

And while you learn the words, don't forget to maintain the *professional attitude*. Nothing is more important. Your professional attitude is the base for implementing both the closing keys *and* the words that make them work better.

CHOOSE WORDS CAREFULLY

The need for using correct words doesn't begin with the close, of course. It starts with the first word in your approach and continues through the last word in your goodbye. However, using right words is more important in the close than any other time because, at the close, the buyer's mind is highly sensitized. He or she is irritable, suspicious, and extremely susceptible to word shadings—more so than at any other time. One wrong word, even one wrong inflection, can kill a sale.

Weigh every word. Use words that build a positive rather than negative reaction in the customer's mind. Get the customer into a *yes* frame of mind. If the buyer gets into the habit of saying *yes* all along it's easier to say *yes* when you ask the important questions. If on the other hand you allow the customer to develop an antagonistic attitude, a *no* outlook, you could lose the sale on attitude alone.

Select your questions carefully to generate a positive response. For example:

"You like the pattern, don't you?" you ask.

"Yes," the customer says.

"This is a very valuable feature, don't you think?"

"Yes."

"You are perhaps wondering just what this attachment does, aren't you?"

The answer nearly always is: "Yes, I have been."

"This would go well with the drapes in your dining room, wouldn't it?"

"Yes, it would."

With these questions as models, phrase a series of questions covering your product or service. By asking questions during the sale, you can build a series of favorable responses. Condition your customer's mind to successful closing.

Some words have power to make or block a sale. Take the simple word *if*. Good closers try to avoid letting *if* into the conversation. It has a negative connotation and too readily leads to a negative response. A much better word to us is *which*.

"*Which* of these two finishes do you prefer?" is a stronger and safer closing phrase than "Shall I send one of these cabinets to your home?"

Use S.O.S.—Something Or Something. Avoid S.O.N.— Something Or Nothing.

In influencing others, certain words have proved extraordinarily powerful. Great trial lawyers, evangelists, and sales leaders collect and use these words. They are not difficult. In fact, they are, without exception, simple common, everyday words. Every closer will find them invaluable.

ALWAYS ASK WHY

Without *why* expert closers say their work would be much harder—sometimes impossible. Imagine you're a buyer. *Why* is hard to answer without committing yourself. Yet it's inoffensive. Children are forever asking *why* of parents. We're used to it. Great salespeople use *why* whenever the sale gets on shaky ground.

Suppose your customer says: "I do not think this is exactly what I want."

Your best defense is: "Why?"

Suppose the customer says: "Oh, I don't know. I just don't think I want it." If you smile, you can ask *why*?

Repeat the word, with charm, to draw out the real reason the customer is hesitating.

During the sale there are often moments when the customer hesitates. You ask: "*Why* do you ponder, Mr. Rinker?"

Or: "*Why* do you think that is true?"

Or: "*Why* do you want to wait until after April 15, when the price will inevitably advance before that time?"

Don't forget that little word *why*—it's one of the most powerful selling and closing words in the rich American language.

A psychologist in Chicago has carried the sales use of *why* to a higher degree. He calls it The Bounce-Back Why. You merely use *why* on the prospect after she throws her *why* at you.

You asked the buyer for an order. The buyer counters: "Why should I buy these goods now?" Use the Bounce-Back: *"Why* do you ask why should you place an order now?" Even against the word why, the most powerful defense is still another *why*.

Remember the schoolyard doggerel:

Y Y U R

Y Y U B

I NO U R

Y Y 4 ME

It translates, as you probably recall:

Too wise you are

Too wise you be

I know you are

Too wise for me

It'll help you recall the power of two *whys* in closing sales.

LET'S USE LET'S

Good closers use *let's* to bring the buyer to buying.

"Let's is highly useful," one ace salesperson explained, "because it's a cooperative word. It's you-and-I-together word. It is an unselfish word. You say to buyers, 'Let's do so and so' and they don't feel coerced. They think it's as much their idea as yours.

"I might say to a woman: 'Let's see why you'll get more for your money if you okay this today.' See how much more effective and acceptable it is than the dogmatic statement: 'You'll get more for your money if you buy today.' The idea is the same. But that word *let's* makes it more acceptable."

This salesperson, whose earnings are in six figures, continued:

"I often say to a prospect, as a strong powerful closing shove: 'Let's arrange for you to try this in your own home.' Make the effort to build closing phrases around *let's*. It's much more effective than the same ideas expressed in other words."

CONNOTE OR DENOTE?

One good salesman started his presentation with: "I'm going to show you *how* this will save you money." This statement is infinitely better than: "You will save money if you install this." *How* arouses curiosity, one of the mind's dominant characteristics.

If a saleswoman tells you she's going to show you how such a thing works, your curiosity is immediately aroused. You want to hear the rest.

Look at the cover headlines on best-selling newsstand magazines. Note frequent use of *how* in headlines. Harness this same power in your selling.

Another magic closing word is *truth*.

"The truth is such and such," a salesperson says. *Truth* immediately gets attention.

"Here is the truth about the situation, Mr. Roberts," a saleswoman says in launching a successful close. *Truth* is strong. It stands for a quality we all respect.

Right is a powerful closing word. Robert D. Esseks, a master seller of leasing services to business, employed it to great advantage. In leasing, the interest rate is, of necessity, arrived at after back-and-forth negotiation. Yet the prospect often asks "What's the rate?" at the beginning.

Esseks always said: "Whatever's *right*!" The prospect invariably relaxed. After all, isn't every buyer interested in the *right* price?

Esseks closed dozens of leasing contracts at the *right* price.

William E. Bolster, an advertising agency account manager, also used the word *right*—in another way. When a client threatened to cut his budget, Bolster told him seriously: "This isn't *right*."

The client reconsidered. After all, if it's not *right*, who wants to do it? Forestalling a cutback saves reclosing the sale all over again later.

Every word has two meanings. The dictionary meaning of words is *denotation:* for example, a dog is a quadruped of the canine species. The second meaning of words, *connotation*, is that peculiar and personal interpretation based on our own experience. Dog means *your* dog, a *neighbor's* dog, a dog *you owned*, a dog that *recently bit you*. You interpret dog and give it your inner meaning. In selling, *connotation* is far more important than *denotation*.

In closing a sale, if you tell the customer to *sign here*, the connotation is formal, legal, formidable, binding, fearful. The buyer has been warned about signing contracts, wills, waivers. The connotation frightens the buyer.

On the other hand, if you suggest that the buyer give you his or her name and address, the buyer isn't afraid. He or she readily and willingly does as you suggest. There are no fearful connotations about those words.

RESPECT WORDS

Many sales have been bungled by a few improperly chosen last-minute words urging the customer to sign. The straw-hat era salesperson disdained such refinements. He or she browbeat customers, saying: "Sign your name right there on the dotted line."

But customers, by not signing in droves, made such salespeople and their methods obsolete. Today we use refined but powerful asking phrases such as:

- "Just your name and address, please."
- "Would you mind looking this over, and if it's correct, put down your name on the next to the last line?"
- "Just write your name and address the way you want it to appear on our records."

Joseph Conrad, the novelist, was an effective user of words. What a salesman he would have been! Conrad had a keen perception of human emotions and respect for the fine shades of difference in word meanings.

A friend suggested that Conrad write an autobiography. Conrad refused. He didn't believe he had anything to say in a life story.

Then his friend insisted: "You know, you really *must.*"

"It was not an argument, but I submitted at once," said Conrad. *"If one must!* You perceive the force of a word. He who wants to persuade should put his trust *not* in the right arguments but in the right *word.* The power of sound has always been greater than the power of sense. Nothing...affecting a whole mass of lives has come from reflection.

"On the other hand, you cannot fail to see the power of mere words, such words as *glory,* for instance, or *pity.* Shouted with perseverance, with ardor, with conviction, these two by their sounds alone have set whole nations in motion and upheaved the dry hard ground on which rests the whole social fabric.

"Of course, the accent must be attended to. The right accent. That's very important. Don't talk to me of your Archimedes lever. Give me the *right* word and the *right* accent and I will move the world!"

An illustration of "give me the right word and the right accent and I will move the world" came during the world's fair. A perfect salesman was at work outside a concession. He was in complete charge for each instant during his presentation. He made the crowd do exactly what he wanted it to do. It was masterful salesmanship.

During a lull, I asked him how many times a day he gave his presentation.

"Five times an hour, twelve hours a day."

"Sixty times a day?"

"That's right."

"Have you been giving it long?"

"Three years."

Each time he gave that talk—without ever changing a word or altering an accent since both were perfect—he made 20 sales. He gave it 60,000 times and made nearly one and a half million individual sales. And the talk contained exactly 237 words.

"I didn't write the talk," he said. "The customers did. I tried telling them and watched results. Whenever I'd think of an improvement, I'd try that. Some worked. Some didn't. Whenever I found a word or phrase that increased sales, I added it. In time, I got a presentation that really brought them in. That's what I wanted.

"Every word in that talk is important. I wouldn't change one word for $500. I couldn't afford to. I'd lose money."

The right words are golden.

One hard-bitten sales executive was a respecter of words. He lacked Conrad's finesse but what he said about words will live long after Conrad's fine words are forgotten. Each morning he said:

"Worship words, you fellows. If you ever stop using 'em right, you stop eating. Remember that."

MASTER OF WORDS

What's the best way to make sure you have the right word at your tongue tip all the time? Wilfred J. Funk, who spent his life among words, believed "the man or woman who's master of words is likewise a master of people." You can acquire word mastery.* Dr. Funk's four suggestions are particularly helpful to salesfolk interested in closing more sales.

Listen to cultured people. Hear them on TV and radio. Hear them at lectures, at church, in conversation with learned men and women. Listen. Notice how they choose their words and how they use them.

Spend 15 minutes a day in serious reading, not comic books or mysteries, but classics—books by word masters.

Look up new words. When you encounter a new word, look it up at once.

Add two new words to your vocabulary every day. Learn their meanings. Use them in writing or speaking several times, until they are yours.

---

*Two excellent word books by A.F. Sisson (Parker Publishing Company, Inc., West Nyack, NY) are *Sisson's Word and Expression Locater* (1966) and *Sisson's Synonyms; An Unabridged Synonym and Related-Terms Locater* (1969).

Salespeople who pay strict attention to the right word **win** confidence and the liking of others. Such men and women **also** close more sales.

Don't be held back by a crippled vocabulary. Study **words** so you use the right one in all your selling conversations.

Edward J. Hegarty, a sales presentation specialist, con-tends—and who is to tell him no—that if a salesperson **learns** to pick the right word and use it in the right way, he or she **can** move the world. But get the *right* word. Here's how **Hegarty** builds a presentation. You can use the same format in **selecting** the right word for your selling presentation.

List the physical features of your product. Translate **each** into a short statement of fact, emphasizing value to the pros-pect. Arrange statements in logical sequence.

Next, write them down. You're going to practically memo-rize them. So get them onto paper.

Write as you talk, naturally.

Don't use *write* words. Use *talk* words.

Say *do* rather than *accomplish, find out* rather than *ascertain,* *go with* instead of *accompany, buy* instead of *purchase, use* rather than *utilize.*

Cut every word you can. Telegraph, don't write. **Deliver** your carefully prepared words like the old gangbuster shows— bang, bang, bang! Your job is to bowl the prospect over, **keep** him awake, keep him with you.

You can hardly overuse questions, those great testers **of** attention. Interlace your presentation with questions. If **you** suspect you're losing the prospect's interest, bring **out a** question to regain it.

When you have the complete presentation worked out **to** your safisfaction, start giving it—time and time again—until you're delivering it with the poise and confidence of an **actor.** After all, you are a skilled business actor, a skilled **user of** words.

AVOID POMPOUS CLICHÉS

Whatever you do, avoid the tired, the hackneyed, **the fad** figure of speech. Don't tell your customers, "Have a good **day!"**

Why be the 14th to say this before 10:30 a.m.? That's not the way to close sales. It only makes you sound like an unimaginative moron.

Peter Hockstein, vice-president of Ogilvy and Mather, New York, has some words for salespeople on use of words: "The following inputs," said the account executive fresh out of business school, "should be sufficient for you to generate a sales presentation."

What he meant to say, of course, was "Here's the information you need to write the presentation."

Here's how to get so gobbledygooked you'll be sure to be *mis*understood:

1. *Use buzzwords* from the mathematical and computer sciences, misapplied to business, words like *parameters*, *inputs*, and *generate*. Instead of saying: "Let's make up a prospect list," say: "Let's input a probability sequence within firmly limited parameters."

2. *Use nouns as verbs.* Example: "The cancer scare will impact our market."

3. *Use gobbledygook.* Here are well-known quotes rendered in gobbledygook. See if you can translate them back to the American language.

I would optimumly prefer to proceed from confirmed models in the decision-making process than to have the Chief Executive Officer's options to implement decisions. *(I'd rather be right than be President.)*

Hopefully, if they input their caloric requirements with pre-sweetened high-yeast-content baked goods products, they will have an affirmative nutritional experience of adequate dimensions. *(Let them eat cake.)*

I am faced with the options of continuing to function as an entity or to abort the process and terminate all operations. *(To be or not to be: that is the question.)*

Proceeding according to acceptable strategy, and on the basis of visual inputs, I launched the strike potential under my authority, thereby effectively relegating the manned enemy subsurface vehicle to a condition of permanent downtime. *(Sighted sub, sank same.)*

All male heads of household have an inherent right under established common law principles to an upscale, multileveled, primary dwelling unit of impermeable construction, accessed by implementing a retractable passageway across an aqueous perimeter. *(A man's house is his castle.)*

At 2 a.m. this morning, a battalion-sized unit of colonial infantry cold-bloodedly launched an aggression against several unprepared and unprotected civilian hamlets and are now proceeding without the support of the oppressed indigenous population, evidently intent on subjugating the legitimate democratic aspirations of marginal agri-businessmen and small commercial enterpreneurs. *(The Redcoats are coming! The Redcoats are coming!)*

As a manager of this functional aggressive marine combat entity, I have decided that we should continue standard operating procedures for combative maneuvers under favorable conditions, despite questionable projections regarding our success. *(Don't give up the ship.)*

Get the point? The phrases are famous because they *move* people to actions, to meet objectives, to do the bidding of celebrated motivators. Which versions are best for closing sales? You know the answer.

TURN-OFF WORDS

You've seen how certain words are a real turn-on. Conversely, other words are turn-offs—not only do they fail to push your case forward, they actually set you back.

Topping the list of turn-offs is *you know*. This fad has reached gigantic proportions. One teenager was heard telling another: "You know, I don't know, you know."

You know between every few words is deadly. For a salesperson, it's murder.

One salesman was heard recently using the phrase "to be honest with you" four times in one presentation. His prospect aptly said: "Anybody who keeps saying, 'To be honest with you,' scares me. What else is he supposed to be but honest?"

Hopefully at the start of most sentences is wrong. In its current fad use, *hopefully* is substituted (grossly and ungrammatically) for *it is hoped*. Since when do effective salespeople say "it is hoped you'll place the order today"? Even correctly employed, the passive voice isn't the selling voice. When used as an introductory, it marks you as a Cliché-Mongering Clod. People don't buy from CMCs.

Frankly inserted in front of each sentence is just as bad. It makes the prospect wonder if it *is* candid.

Other variations that should be avoided are: *to be truthful, honestly speaking, to tell you the truth.* Does a spoken assurance of honesty ever ring true?

Then there is the statement: "I only want a minute or two of your time." If you have anything of value to offer, how can you possibly present it in a minute or two? And how about "I doubt this will interest you. . . ." No, it wouldn't.

Wordiness is a *liability* that afflicts many. The heavy use of superlatives and adjectives. Taking 15 minutes to say what could be simply and better said in 3 minutes. It bores or irritates prospects. Customers aren't impressed by unusual words. The educated person appreciates simplicity in speech. A smart salesperson builds a presentation around clear simple words and statements anyone can understand. Let terminology fit the slow thinker as well as the fast. A person won't buy what he or she doesn't understand.

If you aren't sure of your speech, tape your presentations. If you don't like what you hear, join a public speaking class. Good speech is a mark of the selling professional.

PRACTICE ELOQUENCE

Not every salesperson can be an orator, of course, or even a modern spellbinder. However, you can study speech and improve your vocal presentation.

Practice this customer oration from Bruce Barton, the second founding *B* in BBDO, the New York advertising agency. Barton used it to keep U.S. Steel from canceling its institutional advertising budget.

"Gentlemen, you can cancel your national advertising—that is, if you mean canceling the limited fraction of your advertising you originate and place.

"But the overwhelming fact is that today neither you nor any other big corporation can really halt its advertising. You can only suspend the small part over which you have control.

"The part you do not and cannot control will roll on in ever-increasing volume. It is the advertising given you by politicians with axes to grind, by demagogs who may point you out as typical of all that is bad in big business, by newspapers that hope to build circulation by distorting your acts, by labor leaders misrepresenting your profits, by all other operators in the field of public opinion, some unfriendly and many merely misinformed.

"Thus you are going to have national advertising whether you want it or not!

"The only question you have to decide is whether it is worth a little money, a fraction of one percent of your annual sales, for advertising of your company that will be factual, informative and constructive.

"Or whether, in the present state of world politics, where the electorate is the court of final appeal in ALL business decisions, you can afford to take the risk of having all your advertising emanate from sources beyond your control."

Memorable words, properly applied, close sales. Make sure your word power is first-rate.

THE MASTER CLOSER
IN ACTION

24

CHARLTON HESTON once said the actor has three (and only three) assets—voice, body, and personality. But what powerful tools when employed by a true professional! With voice tone, stage presence, and body language, the skilled thespian moves the audience to laughter or tears—transports you to another time and place or into another person's psyche.

The unusually effective performer (recall Hal Holbrook as *Mark Twain Tonight* on the stage or George C. Scott as *Patton* on the screen) can play the audience like an instrument.

Master closers of sales, like performers, use classic techniques again and again. You must master the keys in this book until they become extensions of yourself. Make them second nature. Soon closing becomes reflex. In time, as you move into a closing situation, the correct keys emerge almost automatically.

One ace salesman calls it "putting yourself in overdrive." Make the closing keys you've mastered part of your business personality. Then when they're needed, they'll emerge at the right time, in the right way.

THE INTEGRATED CLOSER

Bruce Alexander, the California real estate expert, believes the ace closer integrates many major and minor keys into an *overall attitude.*

Closing is the sharp difference between the trained professional and the order taker, according to Alexander. A closer plans ahead to control the sale. In real estate, always take the prospect to see property in your car. Always *your* car. Don't be chintzy and think you're going to save gas by going in the prospect's car. You have no control in their car. *They* can decide when they've seen enough. Keep control.

Take the best route to the property. Don't drive by vacant lots and eyesores. Choose the most scenic route to the property. This is part of your close.

Don't spend valuable drive-out-time in idle chatter. Spend that time talking about the property's *disadvantages,* such as, "It's an excellent value but needs painting inside and outside."

If you *don't* mention that en route, the buyers are going to mention it to *you* when they get there. Take that ammunition away from them.

Say: "Don't be surprised if the front lawn needs landscaping. But other than that, it's a terrific buy." Tell them the negatives, Alexander says.

If you are going to show a property that's a real mess, make it a bigger mess. Say: "The walls have got this and the carpet needs this and the lawn is this high. Oh wow, it really needs an awful lot of work. It's in terrible condition. But I'll tell you this. It's about $6000 under the normal market price. It's a fantastic buy, if you don't mind fixing it up."

Exaggerate the mess. When they get there, they're all excited about the terrific price. When they see the property, they'll say:

"You know it's not *that* bad."

If you don't tell them in advance, they're going to spend the next 15 minutes bending your ear about the fortune it's going to cost to fix it up. Anticipating objections and heading them off is part of the closing attitude.

When you're showing property, get prospects to tell you *then* and *there* anything they don't like. If you don't know the answer and the seller is home, go in the other room and get the answer.

Sense what turns them on the most—the fabulous den, the lovely kitchen, the patio. After they see it all, wander back to that high-appeal spot. Make their last memory the best memory.

Don't forget to isolate a feature and let the buyers sell it back to you. This is a sophisticated closing technique. You've just gone through the property. You've pointed out the built-in range and garbage disposal. You know there's a built-in dishwasher, but you *don't* point that out. Play stupid. Say:

"Gee, Tom and Mary, this property has all the features you wanted, lovely den, complete modern kitchen, just about everything. Wait a minute. I don't remember if it has a built-in dishwasher. Did you notice that, Mary?"

Let her say to you: "Oh, yes, it does."

If she didn't notice, let her go back into the kitchen and say to you: "Hey, it *does* have a built-in dishwasher. It even has that!"

Save something they can sell to you. Let them say: "It *does* have the heater. There *is* a fireplace in the master bedroom."

When they start selling you, you're ready to close.

Start closing by writing up the deal as soon as possible. It's never too soon. Do it in the living room if the seller isn't home.

Write it up on your car fender, or in the car, or wherever you can. Don't drive all the way back to the office—only to find out somebody sold the property ten minutes earlier.

The most basic of all closings is the contract close. Simply ask questions and start filling out the contract. When it's complete, get the prospect to okay it, and you've closed the sale.

If the buyer is not sold enough to go right to contract, use the balance sheet close. Your buyer's straddling the fence. He likes the property, but you just can't nail him down. Say: "Tom and Mary, I want you to do something smart investors do before they make decisions."

Your prospect thinks: "Smart buyers do it. I want to be a smart buyer. I'll do it."

Take a piece of paper and draw a line right down the middle. Say:

"Let's write on this half of the paper all the reasons for *owning* this property. On this side, we'll write down the reasons you should *not* own this property." Help the prospect fill out the sheet.

"The property certainly suits your needs, doesn't it?

"Gee, I like the property." Write that down. *Property suits needs.*

When you finish, the positives should outweigh the negatives three or four to one.

When you're finished, ask the prospect where the preponderance of the evidence lies. That's impressive, the preponderance of the evidence. He or she is going to judge the evidence.

Convert all *general* objections to *specifics*. General: "I want to think it over." Ask: "What parts concern you?" Get the prospect to say: "I'm concerned about the lack of a second bedroom." Now that's an objection you can *work* on.

Now suppose you cannot close. The buyer has a legitimate question. You can answer it tomorrow but not today.

Say it's 2 o'clock in the afternoon. You don't want Tom and Mary to look at any other broker's property today. Somebody may sell them. You want them to go right home.

On the way back, stop and get ice cream. Say: "I'd like you to have this little gift. The kids have been so great. They'll enjoy it."

Now there's ice cream in the car. They *must* go home before it melts. When they get home and give the kids the ice cream, they're not going to feel like going out again. They're off the market until you're ready for them the next day. That's a closing attitude.

If you go back to the office, and your prospect is parked in back, you park in front so they must come through the office. Get them in and go into the closing. If you drive up near their car, they'll get in and they're gone. Plan ahead like a closer.

Good closers are not born. Closers develop themselves. That's what makes a professional. Practice, perfecting your craft. Now if you're in real estate, you undoubtedly recognize the touch of the master's hand. But no matter what you sell, you can benefit from the example. Notice how the closing keys are so integrated they're almost invisible—but all the more effective for being non-obvious.

Put this closing advice under the microscope, and you'll begin to see some of the closing keys emerge.

The *Little Question* appears several times, not overt, but interwoven. In three places, he gets the prospect to answer questions that advance the sale.

Do Something. He gets the prospect to write advantages and disadvantages and then make the final judgment.

Third Party Endorsement. Who better than the prospects themselves? Let *them* tell *you* how wonderful it is.

Something for Nothing. The ice cream. But it comes with a double-whammy: they must get it home quickly and cannot see a competitive property.

Closing keys are there, if you look for them, and all the more powerful because they're integrated. They may be closing keys to you, but to the buyer, they're reassuring advice, or helpful information that performs a real service. When your closing keys become second nature, they *will* be interwoven in much that same manner, no matter what product or service you sell.

Of course, in some selling situations, the keys are more overt, as this classic sale by David Boue illustrates.

DAVE BOUE'S VISIBLE CLOSING KEYS

Dave Boue arrives at the sale fully prepared to use any (or all) of his carefully orchestrated closers.

"What I use depends on what the prospect says or does," Boue says.

Does this mean Boue eschews homework and plays it by ear? Absolutely not. He sells a complicated business service in a volume of $200,000 a year. This requires intensive preparation. He must know his service inside-out, know the client's business, and know his closing keys.

"I'm prepared to draw on any of 25 responses," Boue says. "I don't know which I'll need, but it doesn't matter. I'm ready."

Does that sound like an enormous amount of work? Yes. But it pays off in spades or, more properly, in dollars. Watch Dave Boue at work.

Boue is calling on Whitelaw Chambers, general manager of a company that makes solar products for the home. Boue sells a seminar service that dramatizes product benefits to the public. It's intangible, new to many prospects, and hard to grasp.

This is Boue's second call. On his first call, he left Chambers a plan and budget.

Boue arrives at Chambers' office at 8:45 a.m.— "the day gets complicated as it wears on at that company." (Before meeting Chambers, Boue stopped in to see Chambers' boss, Gorgeson Reilly, to make a valuable suggestion on a *completely unrelated* matter.) He's now seated with Chambers.

"Coffee?" Chambers asks.

"No, thanks," Boue says. "I brought my own." From his briefcase, he takes a small compact coffeemaker and small silver cup. "I have special blend made in Brazil. Want to try mine?"

In wonder, Chambers does.

"Very appropriate we should be talking about solar products today, Whitelaw," Boue says. "I was just reading this article in *The New York Times* last Sunday. It relates directly to the future of your business."

Naturally, Chambers is interested. (It's amazing how many business executives have *not* read key articles," Boue says. "I use this to advantage.")

Boue summarizes the *Times* comments. Solar products, once considered a novelty, are now a necessity to many consumers. When it comes to saving energy, people don't worry about whether to install a solar device—they concentrate on *how* to get it.

"So this is the solar year," Boue says. "But as you know better than I, you're in an ease-of-entry business. Almost anyone can set up in a garage and call himself a solar products manufacturer. The number of companies in the field has grown by 500 percent in the past year, according to the Solar Products Association. There's a power struggle going on right now for leadership in the consumer's mind. A few will emerge as leaders in the public mind. Many more will be left by the wayside and go out of business."

Chambers nods. What Boue is saying is certainly provocative.

"To establish leadership, your company must make a dramatic but legitimate gesture," Boue says. "Now it's true you put on a public demonstration about 18 months ago when the industry was much younger. And you've benefited from that. But you must decide when you can be on the *give* and when you can be on the *take*."

Give? Take? How does that work, Chambers wants to know.

Here Boue stops the action (seemingly) to tell Chambers a story. When Nelson Rockefeller was running for re-election as governor of New York, some of his political enemies circulated rumors that Rockefeller was on the *give* politically—that he was giving money to certain groups to swing votes his way come election day.

"This contrasts with the usual political charge of being on the *take*," Boue says. "Naturally it wouldn't be credible to accuse a Rockefeller of being on the *take*. Who could offer him money that he doesn't already have? So they accused him of being on the *give*."

Chambers, who follows politics closely, is amused by the story.

"On the *give*," he says. "That's pretty good."

But that's a moral here, Boue says, that applies to the solar industry. (In one deft stroke, he shifts back to closing the sale).

"When you made that public demonstration 18 months ago," Boue says, "you were on the *give*—giving the public information and instruction to help buyers make decisions about solarizing homes. People appreciate that. When they get ready to buy, they turn—in many cases—to that helpful company that put on the demonstration."

Since that time, Boue tells Chambers, your company has been on the *take*.

"You've been reaping the benefits of that early demonstration," Boue says. "But you cannot go on being on the take forever. Now you've got to go on the *give* again. This public demonstration is the most dramatic legitimate way to go on the *give*."

Chambers is nearly convinced. However, there's the matter of price.

"Let me pour you another cup of coffee," Boue says," and I'll tell you how we plan to save you money over the previous quote."

Boue then details a plan whereby Chambers can rent a meeting site at less money than before by bartering some of his solar products in exchange for space.

"This will reduce your costs by $2,000," Boue says.

Just then, Gorgeson Reilly comes into Chambers' office.

"Sorry to interrupt," Reilly says. "Just wanted to catch Dave before he left. Dave, that's a good suggestion you made today. We're moving out on it. Thanks a lot."

Naturally, Dave says he's glad to help.

"By the way, Gorgeson," Chambers says. "I want to see you a little later about a new plan for a public demonstration. We want to make a decision on this right away."

Gorgeson agrees and left. Boue asks Chambers to decide *which* products he wants to barter. He then gets Chambers to initial the contract. The sale is closed.

HOW BOUE CLOSED THROUGHOUT

Off the cuff? Far from it. Dave Boue went in loaded for bear. Canned presentation? No. Boue stored a number of *prepared elements* in his mind, but the presentation moved like a skilled performer on a talk show. Boue drew on rehearsed components. He filled in between the bricks with pleasing and convincing conversational mortar.

Ar you willing to prepare to that extent? Do you know your closing keys so well they pop up as needed—almost (but not quite) by reflex? Well, master closers *do*. Let's examine the closing keys Dave Boue drew from mental inventory.

First, he set the time to suit buyer mood (in this case early in the morning) to sell in the right psychological climate. He brought along a distinctive coffee pot and offered his customer a drink from a silver cup (The *Do Something* Key). This insured customer interest. It set Dave aside from any 999 other salespeople Chambers may have known.

Dave was selling an event, so his *Coming Event* Key was built-in. His well-prepared manner assumed he'd get the order (*Beyond Any Doubt* Key). He used Chambers' own boss to get his *Third Party Endorsement*. Of course, Reilly coming in to Chambers' office was a stroke of luck. (Or was it? Good closers make their own luck!)

Boue also used *The Coming Event* Key in talking about the industry shakeout and how some companies will be left by the wayside.

Because he had investigated a less expensive way for Chambers to buy, he was really offering *Something for Nothing*.

Boue even worked in *The Little Question* Key by asking Chambers which products he wanted to barter. Not *if* but *which*—a much easier decision to make.

Of course at the end Boue trotted out *Ask and Get*—time for Chambers to sign. He signed.

Clearly, Boue's most important move was stopping the sale to tell a related story about Nelson Rockefeller. Storytelling is part of the *Third Party Endorsement* Key. But once he told his story, Boue immediately moved back into the close.

He opened with a true story from *The New York Times* about Chambers' industry. You can't hit them harder than that.

In this one close, Boue wove all seven major keys into his presentation. He used a number of special keys—plus much good common sense and good salesmanship. He was *prepared* totally—a true professional at work.

SAME ARSENAL AVAILABLE TO YOU

The seven secret keys and the thirteen special keys to closing sales are now *yours*. Scale them up and down. Adapt and adopt. Rejigger and rebore. Polish and sand. By the time you finish, they won't look like these keys at all. No matter. Use these principles as your launching pad. Where you go beyond that is as wide open as outerspace.

Review what you have learned in this book to make sure it sticks. You started with a rundown on the importance of closing—quite simply, if you cannot close, you cannot sell. There are no born closers. Closing can be learned. Take your instruction from the world's champion closers.

You learned the importance of building a foundation. Dave Boue started working on his close when he read *The New York Times* article and decided to use it as ammunition. (Correction. He started his close by keeping informed in the first place!)

Your foundation includes being able to speak clearly, colorfully, and persuasively—the closer's *fundamental* tools. If you're not an expert speaker, start studying. You must master the language before doing anything else.

DEVELOP CLOSING RADAR

Champions develop a sixth sense about when to close. No two sales are alike. When in doubt, try to close: it can't hurt and often works. Through a process known as autoconditioning, tune your mind to *think closing*—always be alert to opportunity, always move in when opportunities arise, no matter where or when they occur.

Get your own mind in shape first. Dump negative baggage. Sell "you" to yourself and then to others. Live with the principle that knowledge is power.

Learn *when* to listen and *how* to listen. The right kind of listening is golden.

Know when to make a strategic withdrawal. Don't beat your head against a wall. Go away. Come back with new ammunition and try again. Take a different tack. Remember how Bob Carl sold H. L. Hunt, the world's richest man.

Never think you know it all. Even 25-year-pros still practice closing presentations every day. So must you, if you continue to make progress.

TURNING WEAKNESS INTO STRENGTH

Every buyer has an Achilles' heel. Always attack where the defense is weakest. This means understanding personality types as analyzed by social scientists. The more you know about human vulnerability, the better you close sales. Closely related: arrange to close in the right psychological climate as Dave Boue did.

As Bob Shiffman proved in selling Cadillacs, you're never wrong to assume the prospect is money-minded. Convert your product or service to a money-advantage, and you're well on your way to closing.

Let the prospect tell you when to close—by words, via body language, by buying signals.

You picked up the master closing formula: every call is a closing opportunity. Try to close early and on every buyer resistance. Keep trying time after time.

Background in hand, you moved into the seven secret closing keys.

Remember how Mehdi used *Beyond Any Doubt* selling the two partners Tony and Tom.

Hubert Bermont's use of *The Little Question* was interesting: he merely asked the customer why he was hesitating to buy.

Who can forget the manufacturer who used the *Do Something* Key and encouraged the customer to autograph the product with a big blue pencil?

The *Coming Event* is powerful. Dick Considine showed you how to create your own coming event.

Letting others sell for you is what the *Third Party Endorsement* is all about. If you can tell this in story form, so much the better. Everybody likes stories.

The buyer who doesn't respond to *Something for Nothing* has not been born yet. Remember what Al Wall did with free advice. As Henry Ford I said to his neighbor who sold insurance: "You didn't ask me." *Ask and Get* and you'll close an amazing number of times.

Seldom will you use all seven keys as Dave Boue did in selling Whitelaw Chambers. But learn when to use what key. And be prepared to use any key as the need arises.

YOUR SPECIAL SELLING KEYS

With master keys in hand, you moved on to the special keys—equally valuable in many ways. You learned to give the buyer a choice—something or something. Never something or nothing.

Don't be afraid of talking about money. Mention it as casually as possible—cash or check? Appeal to pride: "Imagine how you'll feel using this product!"

If you cannot sell now, make a commitment for the future. Better a later sale than no sale.

When you get knocked out of the box, start to go and then come back to say, "Oh, one more thing." Often that one thing will close.

Every buyer wants special treatment. It can be trivial but it works.

Sometimes the first person to speak loses. Learn when to close with silence.

The special keys are selling's grace notes. Use them in support of the secret keys. They work.

Mark Wright, as you recall, assumes his prospect doesn't understand. He starts his closing presentation all over again. It works. Other closers call this The Balk. They stop the action and start a different topic entirely. The first thing the buyer knows, he or she is back on track, writing the order.

Built into the major and special keys is a power quality that keeps recurring time and again—persistence. Successful closers always try one more time.

Once the customer is signed, you learned two important principles: nail down the sale so it stays closed (thank the customer, reassure him on the wisdom of his decision) and then get out. Don't linger to give him time for second thoughts.

For every rule there's an exception: remember how Ellery Jordahl *stayed* for dinner long after the sale was closed because he felt it had closed *too* fast? He wanted to solidify it with empathy and sharing of common farming experience.

As valuable as these closing keys are, and as often as they work, nothing works all the time. Sometimes the buyer still says: "Nothing doing, and I mean it." Here the seasoned closer opts for strategic retreat and is soon back again to start over.

Another option: get tough—when you have nothing to lose. Remember what George Garmus did with the buyer who'd never get off the telephone.

Tom O'Ryan did it by being a young-and-innocent who didn't know you couldn't keep coming back day after day. Both approaches will work many times.

The appeal to humanity sells many orders—as Paul Meyer proved with his bumbling speech. Empathy, as Ellery Jordahl proved, is a valuable closing tool. Use empathy to close The Chatterbox and The Clam—both extreme buyer types—and others in between.

Use sympathetic listening to flatter your buyer. Real estate ace O.C. Halyard replies to every question with a question—and his prospects buy in droves.

You capped out your closing understanding with a look at power words—the components that make your speech golden and your pocket green.

Power words motivate, captivate, and titillate your prospect. Power words place your prospect in a Yes mood. Most are simple words, including *which* (something or something), *why* (the favorite of all great closers), *what if* (the fantasy spinner's workhorse), *let's* (remember Lyndon Johnson's Biblical quotation: "Come, let us reason together"), *here's how* (this will save you money or time), *right* (everyone wants to do what is right), and many more.

Seasoned closers use *talk* words, not *write* words. You must also avoid clichés and fad phrases that label you as "non-think."

There you have it: a complete collection of closing advice and experience from the best salespeople in America.

CONTINUE TO USE THIS REFERENCE

Classics *are* classic because they can be experienced time and again with increasing value. H. L. Mencken said: "Everyone who loves music should hear Bach's Mass in B Minor at least once a year." So it is with this collection of closing techniques.

Once you make the closing keys part of your nature, you'll close the easy sales and medium-hard sales automatically.

Use this book as a reference whenever you face a knotty new problem. No matter what your need, there's advice or experience here that will help. Re-read this book once a year to reinforce your closing knowledge.

The purpose of *Secrets of Closing Sales* is to make your work easier, more productive, more profitable, and—perhaps most important of all—more fun. You now have the tools to do just that. Good selling! And remember: good closers make their own luck.

INDEX